At Hamburg Inn

the line of customers

forms at the cash register

and winds its way

outside,

down the street,

to the highway,

and beyond

At Hamburg Inn

let's begin

with the burger of truth

and the fries of logic

At Hamburg Inn

I ask Adam

for a refill of coffee

"Regular?" he says

"I'd prefer irregular."

At Hamburg Inn

"Just Eggs"

are on the breakfast menu

They come with

just bacon

just toast

just hash browns

just orange juice

and just about

anything else you want

They're just delicious

At Hamburg Inn

The hot dogs

bark

in the summer

At Hamburg Inn

I am snapping

word pictures

with my

poetry camera

At Hamburg Inn

everyone speaks

Innglish

At Hamburg Inn

each table

smiles

when a customer

sits down

on one of

its chairs

At Hamburg Inn

there are two doors

One for you

and one for you

At Hamburg Inn

I pour syrup

on french fries

and catsup

on pancakes

because

I'm colorblind

At Hamburg Inn

they have the Kids Fun Meal

to go with the Grown-ups Laughter Meal

which are served

by Smiley Face People

At Hamburg Inn

a man reads the newspaper

and a woman reads the menu

while their young daughter reads

"The Brothers Karamazov"

The Burg
A Writers' Diner

Marybeth Slonneger

By Hand Press
2011

When sandwiches were 5¢—Joe Panther is in the window on the left, his sister Bernedette is on the far right, man in center is unknown.

Copyright © 2011 by Marybeth Slonneger

ISBN 978-0-9672242-2-0

By Hand Press
1109 Davenport Street
Iowa City, IA 52245
mbslonn@mchsi.com

Any profit from the sale of this book will be donated to the Johnson County Heritage Trust whose mission is "the preservation and enjoyment of natural areas primarily in Johnson County. These include prairies, woodlands, wetlands and sites of historic, archeological or scenic interest, as well as easements on properties not accessible to the general public."

Earliest known photograph of Hamburg Inn No. 1

"We're the brown-bag, plain-vanilla type of place," said owner Dave Panther. Jennings, Cedar Rapids Gazette, 2003

Leona and Bernadine Panther, the sisters of Adrian, Fritz, and Joe; Joe is probably in the window, circa 1938

—T 'n' T—
THERE WAS A YOUNG
FELLOW NAMED WIMPY
Who found most
'burgers quite
skimpy
Till the day he
dropped in
At the great
HAMBURG INN
No hamburg had ever filled
Wimpy.

TIPS'N'TATTLES
Iowa City Press-Citizen
Tuesday, September 16, 1941

To those who love the Hamburg Inn
and to the community that nurtures it
and to Gary, who inspired the book

The Hamburg Inn story began in the mid 1930s when Joe Panther started Hamburg Inn on Iowa Avenue. His brother Adrian eventually joined Joe. Hamburgers sold for a nickel, there were 10 burgers to the pound and they gained the nickname 'grease spots.'

Dave Panther, *Burg Diner Liner*, July 2008

Watercolor sketch of Hamburg Inn No.1 by Niles Vaught, who worked at the Burg, 1970s

The vacant building to the left had once housed the Athens Press; by 1938, it was the Iowa City Recreation Center; it became Strickford Campus Supplies in 1942 but was vacant a year later; Paris Cleaners had moved in by 1946.

Here's how the Hamburg Inn in Iowa City looked in 1937.

Neighbors photo courtesy of David Par

Guest Contributors

Larry Baker
Marvin Bell
Ralph Cap
Jeff Charis-Carlson
Mary Jo Dane
John Deeth
Biswamit Dwibedy
Hope Edelman
Steve Fugate
Allan Gurganus
Matt Hayek
Paul Ingram
Michael Knock
Cinda Kornblum
Karen Kubby
Thomas Leverett
Jean Lloyd-Jones
Mary Mascher
Robert Garner McBrearty
James Alan McPherson
Dave Morice
Bill Panther
Bob Panther
Dave Panther
Marty Panther
Mary Panther
Roma Panther
Steve Panther
Gary Sanders
Liz Sanders
Morty Sklar
Mary Helen Stefaniak
Mary (Stroh) Swanson
Laurel Synder
Steve Toth
Barbara Yates
A Little History

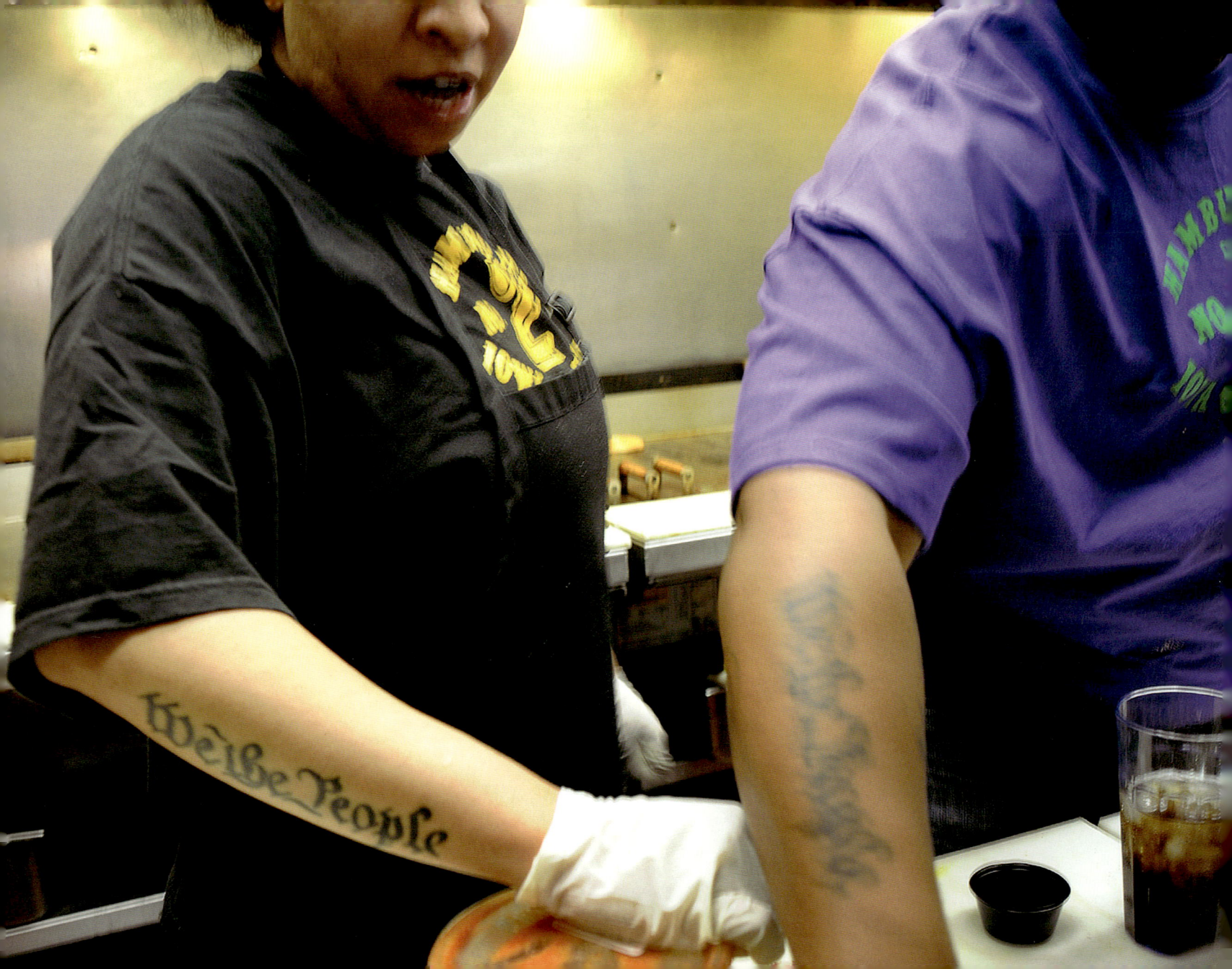

If you stand behind the register as a hostess at the Hamburg Inn, as I had the pleasure of doing, you might be told about college memories from an out-of-towner or chat with a worker who drove fifty miles to Iowa City to sample food that "just doesn't get any better than this."

The Burg is about food that's been served to people for the last sixty-plus years. But it's also about hard work, loyal customers, comfortable surroundings, and finding the expected with each visit. Important visitors have come for a meal, including three presidents, and student servers have earned tuition working here. But what interested me most was that during off moments, sketches were made, notes jotted down, and photos taken (including the ones I took during my shift.) So, I thought of offering a sample of what can be found on the daily menu at the Hamburg Inn through the eyes of its visitors.

Marybeth Slonneger
(I always order the California omelet)

Polly and Paris, two fine cooks

Matt Hayek

Message from the Mayor

Plenty of communities have diners, but few combine local roots with national relevance. For most of us, the Hamburg Inn is a beloved greasy spoon. For presidential candidates, it's a required stop. Iowa City is blessed with institutions – the writers workshop, our hospitals, our football program – that draw attention from around the country. The Hamburg Inn is right up there with them.

Matt Hayek traces his Iowa City roots to roughly 1867, when his Czech ancestors settled in Goosetown. Formerly a Peace Corps volunteer in Bolivia, Matt practices law in addition to serving as mayor of Iowa City. He and his wife have three young children.

" There is only ONE No. 2 " Dave Panther, Owner

Hamburg Inn #1 on the day it closed, May 27, 1978

Jeff Charis-Carlson

Introduction

"Okay boys," long-shot Republican presidential candidate Pat Buchanan said as he and his wife eyed their hamburgers and fries warily, "it's time to turn the cameras off. No pictures while we're eating."

It was 1999, and a coterie of local journalists — with one or two national reporters — formed a half circle around the Ronald Reagan table at Hamburg Inn No. 2. I had just finished asking Buchanan a series of unmemorable questions about his quixotic presidential campaign, but I was far too young of a reporter to realize that I really should have asked him what he thought of the Hamburg.

After all, both Buchanan and his immaculately dressed wife wore thinly disguised looks of confusion, even frustration, as they began to eat their hamburgers with a knife and fork.

"Didn't those campaign guys check out this place before they put it on the schedule?" I imagined Buchanan was thinking before he raised his fork and announced a forceful, "Great burger!"

His wife, sitting in half-smiling silence, probably was asking herself, "Why would there be a table dedicated to Ronald Reagan in a restaurant where the waitresses have pink hair, tattoos and nose rings? Why would a college-town diner be the go-to spot for connecting with potential caucus-goers of any ideological stripe?"

I could understand the Buchanans' confusion that day because I shared it. Although I already had been in Iowa City for six months, I had never before made it into the fabled Hamburg Inn. I had seen the diner across Linn Street during my frequent visits to the Northside Book Market — now The Haunted Bookshop — but those visits were usually too late for breakfast and too early for supper.

And I can't say watching the Buchanans' discomfort was a good recommendation for the quality of the food.

In the past 12 years, of course, the Hamburg Inn really has grown into the essential campaign stop that Buchanan's schedulers recognized it as. The campaigning for the 2004 caucuses not only included frequent stops by the Democratic candidates and their surrogates — including Howard Dean supporter, Martin Sheen — but a Hamburg-esque diner was featured the 2005 "King Corn" episode of the

The #2 neon sign was designed and built by Steve Panther.

Sheen's television series, "The West Wing."

Without a sitting president or vice president campaigning for the 2008 caucuses, candidates from both major parties made regular and highly publicized stops at the Hamburg — often adding their own bean to the restaurant's Coffee Bean Poll. Few of the candidates had the time to stop and eat a meal. And for the heavy hitters, even if they wanted to eat, there seldom was room to sit down.

"It's butt-to-butt in there," second-generation owner Dave Panther said of a visit by Texas Gov. Rick Perry in August of 2011.

The increased political coverage helped the Hamburg gain even more recognition in national travel and food magazines, and the restaurant now is often hailed as a go-to stop for any devotee of American cuisine. The national newspaper and radio stories about the restaurant's pie-shakes, likewise, have become journalistic shorthand for describing the equal parts wholesomeness and kitschiness that Iowa brings to the presidential selection process.

But the past 12 years also have taught me how the local importance of the Hamburg goes back long before that day in 1992 when former President Ronald Reagan ate a meal in the back corner booth and left a very healthy tip. It goes back to when, as Paul Ingram explains, the "servers were not the tattooed art students you find there now," but "grandmothers in their mid-fifties who took their jobs and their customers quite seriously." It goes back to when, as poet Marvin Bell explains, the famous and prestigious Iowa Writers' Workshop "was a bohemian anomaly and vaguely disreputable."

Hamburg Inn No. 2 is now the place in Iowa City I go for breakfast most often. And when I order my coffee, Eggciting Sandwich and a small biscuits and gravy, I partake in a family's comfort food legacy that stretches back not only to 1948, when Fritz and Fran Panther bought out Mrs. Van's Restaurant on North Linn Street, but all the way to the mid-1930s, when Joe Panther opened an unnumbered Hamburg Inn on Iowa Avenue and started selling burgers for 5 cents each.

For more than six decades, Hamburg Inn No. 2 has been a place where your coffee is refilled before you think to ask, where waiters and waitresses are hired on the spot, where the muse is known to strike at any moment, where college students take their parents to tell them shocking news, where mourners see ghosts from the past, and where a good omelet with home fries can take the edge off any hangover.

I'm glad Marybeth Slonneger has been working so hard to preserve the memory of this important Iowa City landmark. I only wish I had been allowed to take a photo of Pat Buchanan eating to add to the collection.

September 26, 2011

Jeff Charis-Carlson is the opinion page editor of the *Iowa City Press-Citizen*.

Dave Panther

My Earliest Memories

My earliest memories of the Hamburg Inn are from living in the apartment above the restaurant. It was mostly the noises and smells. The clatter and clinking of plates and silverware, the occasional loud laughter or talking. The constant humming of the grill exhaust fan with the cooking smells of burgers and bacon. The constant opening of the front and back doors for customers and deliveries. There was an outside porch and stairway on the back the building that Dad and Mom would use and Dad always smelled like fries. He was always up by 4 am and I would sometimes wander into the bathroom while he was shaving when I could just not hold the pee in any longer. He would go down and start the grills and begin making chili, French fries, and American fries for the start of the day. Dad always felt he needed to be on the grill when it was busy and he was very good at greeting and talking to his guests.

On Sunday, Hamburg Inn did not open till 4 pm so all of us kids would have little jobs to do on Sunday mornings. Stocking the pop cooler with bottles, the refrigerator with small cartons of milk and assorted small cleaning jobs. Eventually we worked part time doing dishes before and after school. My brothers and I were among the very few of our fellow friends who had jobs at a very early age to earn spending money. A gift that was both a love and a curse as we grew up.

One of my jobs as I got older and bigger was making all the French fries for Hamburg Inn's 1 and 2 and Big 10 Inn. We had a production set-up in the basement and I would peel and cut 400 to 500 lbs of French fries at a time. We would pre-cook the fries for about 2 to 3 minutes depending on the water content of the potato so that when they were ordered it would not take as long to cook.

Dad always used fresh ground burger which we eventually started grinding ourselves when Dad hired Otto Dolezal. The burger at the time were a quarter pound and hand-rolled into burger balls that we flattened on the grill. Dad bought a pattie-maker one year and used it for 2 days before he sent it back. He felt it changed the texture and taste of the burgers.

When Hamburg Inn opened everything was in the same room. The grills, fryers, steam table and dishwashing station were all on the back wall. There was a 12-stool counter and 5 booths. That was the layout until 1990 when we remodeled. The menu was small with daily homemade specials and on the weekends before the fast food trend we had to set up an extra grill in the back room to handle carry out order.

Dave in his office

Graf Beverage was located where the Hamburg Inn parking is now along the alley. The Graf family also own the Hamburg Inn building and Dad was able to buy it from them in the early 70's. We sold Graf soda pop. Every week they would run different flavors like cream soda, black cherry, root beer. We would always look forward to the delivery to see what new flavors would be in the order. Our delivery man was named Howard and he always had a smile, the local gossip, and the need for some deodorant. Howard eventually worked for my dad and Uncle Adrian when Graf Beverage closed.

Bill Discol was our bread delivery man for over 20 years. He took great pride in his job and always made sure we were well supplied. He also had a great respect and friendship for my dad and mom.

There were many ladies over the years who supervised the Hamburg Inn at night and many had all their children working here part time through high school: Arlen Ellis, Helen Honts, Agnes Loney, are just a few. Dad called them jewels for being such great people and staff. Hamburg Inn has always been successful because of the Great people who have worked here to make it so.

The Hamburg Inn building was heated by a coal furnace for years and as kids we were always fascinated by it. I enjoyed stoking the coal hopper and removing the clinkers from the furnace. They would come out red hot and glowing and look like something from a volcano when they cooled.

We used to shut down for a couple of days after Christmas for deep cleaning of everything and I always remembered it as 2 or 3 days of chaos with the grills, fryers, and grill exhaust system torn apart for cleaning and maintenance. I remember the chicken pressure-fryers as being a nightmare to take apart and put back together. On one of these cleaning adventures I decided to replace the entryway flooring and tile myself. This turned into a never ending battle because of my lack of handyman ability. We ended up being closed for an extra day. When I thought I was finished and went to lock the front door, the door fell off it's hinges. That floor did last the next 10 years though.

I joined Dad in 1975 after I got out of the Air Force and managed Hamburg Inn until 1979 as Dad started to take more time and travel away from the restaurant. In 1979 he was ready to sell and we worked out a buy-out plan and Dad would still drop in to do small jobs when he felt like it. In 1981 Mike joined me in the business and eventually became my partner. Mike was a great addition and was much more outgoing than I was so he related well with both the guests and the staff. But bad stuff happens to us all and Mike was killed by a drunk driver in December of 1985. It's taken a long time to bury the sadness and if I think about it for too long it all comes back.

Hamburg Inn No. 1 opened ... in the heart of the downtown at 119 Iowa Ave... The dinky diner had eight stools and was run by a fellow named 'Pops.' Staff Writer, *Cedar Rapids Gazette,* May 28, 1986

—T 'n' T—

THERE'S A NOOK
WHERE THE COOK
will quickly serve
with much verve
the biggest hamburger in town for a
dime   It's HAMBURG INN where
you should stop for
Folger's coffee fresh and hot
ice cold beverages cigarettes
and sandwiches of all varieties
Stop at HAMBURG INN for a
quick lunch anytime

"In 1938, [Adrain] Panther rented the sandwich shop [on Iowa Avenue]... Hamburgers sold for a nickel then. Five years later, he bought the business for $750. By then his hamburgers were quarter-pounders and sold for a dime. Business at No.1 was good until the speed feed restaurant chains moved into the downtown area here several years ago," Panther said. 'The competition made it harder to get good managers... [the] No.1 business was sold for $7,500 [in 1978]." Heth, *Des Moines Register,* May 1978

Bob Panther

Hamburg Inn #1 History

Adrian Panther [father of Bob Panther] was the youngest child of Frank and Frannie Panther of Mt. Pleasant, Iowa. His three oldest siblings, Bernadine, Leona and Genevieve never left the area, but Adrian and his two older brothers, Joseph and Francis (Fritz), migrated to Iowa City as young men. Adrian left Mt. Wesleyan College for the University of Iowa on a track scholarship, but dropped out of college after a short time to take over the ownership of Hamburg Inn #1. Oldest brother, Joe Panther, had owned the business for awhile with a friend, Maurice Keeley, but Joe returned to Mt. Pleasant for a career in pharmacy. Adrian would remain the sole owner of Hamburg Inn #1 until he and Fritz formed a partnership and opened Hamburg in #2 in 1948.

Adrian often recalled that in 1942, the year I was born, the restaurant wasn't making much money selling 5¢ hamburgers, so as a new father he decided to go to Davenport to look for a job at Alcoa or some other defense-related factory. He stood at the intersection of Burlington and Dodge for two hours trying to hitch-hike a ride but no one stopped for him. With nothing to do but think during those two hours, he decided if he was going out of business, he would go out trying. He would raise the price of hamburgers from a nickel to a dime. He was afraid he would lose all of his customers. "I don't believe I lost a single customer," he would say incredulously every time he told the story.

Dad and Fritz bought Van's Café from Mrs. Van in 1948. The restaurant was still operating and serving Blue Plate Specials until just before remodeling began for the change to Hamburg Inn #2. I was with Dad when Mrs. Van asked what kind of restaurant he was going to have. Dad said it would serve hamburgers and chili, like the one on Iowa Avenue. I remember Mrs. Van saying, "Oh, well, you're going to go broke then, the working people around here need a regular meal for lunch." I was only six years old, but I knew going broke was not a good thing. Dad must have sensed my concern because as we left, he said "All she sees are a few working people eating lunch at her place every day, but what I see when I look around here are students, and students will eat hamburgers every single day."

A typical work day for Dad: up at 4 a.m.; scrub and prep work from 5 to 6 a.m. at the restaurant; open at 6 a.m.; work until about 2 p.m.; come home and take a nap until 4:30 p.m.; return to work until supper hour was over; come home and do a couple of hours of bookwork. He did that six days a week and he did it for years. I never heard him complain about the hours he worked. Dad loved football Saturdays in general, and Homecoming in particular. Besides being incredibly busy, he enjoyed hearing people say they had eaten there 20 years before when they were students, and that the hamburgers were just as good as they remembered. Dad would just beam, and I could tell that was what made his hard work and effort worth it.

Waitresses at No. 1, 1960s

Marvin Bell

Starting from #1

I'm a Writers' Workshop dinosaur, which means I remember Hamburg Inn #1, appropriately located on Iowa Avenue at a time when the Workshop was a bohemian anomaly and vaguely disreputable. Maybe Hamburg Inn #1 was, too, because it felt informal, comfortably ragged in character, utterly charming—not that we noticed the charm. It was, in more ways than one, a place to chew the fat. Most writers are nothing if not oral.

My clearest memory of the Inn is of the cool autumn evening the poet Donald Justice, Annie Searle, who was the secretary and only office employee of what was then a much smaller Writers' Workshop, Larry Barrett, the mellifluous voice of radio station WSUI, and I came out of Kenney's toward midnight. Kenney's was the bar where the writers hung out, as Hamburg Inn #1 was the grill of choice.

The streets were empty as we walked north on Clinton until a dozen or so Iowa football players, led by quarterback Gary Snook, emptied boisterously out of Joe's Place, across the street from us. They were having a beer can fight and one of the cans flew near Justice's parked car. Don objected, to which one of the players yelled F*** You!

Don was noted for a competitive spirit that sometimes took hold at risky moments. (He even wrote a poem about it, addressed to his heart, in which he referred to his impulsive temper and called his heart a "seedy, old pomegranate.") So, naturally, Don yelled back F*** You! with an unmistakable accent on "You."

At this point, as Annie hurried away, Don, Larry and I found ourselves walking across the street to get beat up by the Iowa football team. Once on the opposite sidewalk, standing in front of a few parked cars, I was scouting the group for a safety when one of the smaller guys came up to Larry, who had his hands in the pockets of a large winter coat. He was probably the safety.

"I'm the smallest guy here," he said. "Do you wanna get hit by me?" Larry, in his most deep, mellifluous tones, said, "Well, if you're the smallest guy here, of course I want to get hit by you." At which point, the player hit Larry, who fell backwards and slid down the side of a parked car, all without taking his hands from his pockets and continuing to speak in that warm radio voice of his.

A few moments later we were all in Hamburg Inn #1 with our arms around one another, singing the Iowa Fight Song.

License on car is 1945, the probable time of photograph

Where else could we have gone? It was Hamburg Inn where one could go at all hours. Sure, Inn #1 turned into one of two, and then #2 took over, but it was Inn #1 that established the character of the menu and the service so that Inn #2, whatever its upgrades, would never go white collar or dull. Hamburg Inn #2 is a WYSIWYG kind of place. You see what you get and you get what you see. If it ain't on the menu, you don't need it. And there are people waiting for your table.

May 10, 2011

Poet Marvin Bell came to Iowa City in 1961 to be "graduate student bum" in the Writers' Workshop for three years. After two years in the Army, he returned to Iowa City and taught forty years for the Workshop, retiring in 2005 as Flannery O'Connor Professor of Letters. He also served two years as Iowa's first poet laureate. He has published twenty three books.

No. 2 opened on July 8, 1948

In 1948, Mrs. Van's Restaurant on N. Linn Street came up for sale and was bought by another brother, Fritz Panther and his wife, Fran. Adrian and Fritz formed a partnership and over the years had Hamburg Inn #1 and #2, Big Ten Inn on Riverside Drive and the Airport Inn in Iowa City. They also had Hamburg Inn #3 in Cedar Rapids on Center Point Road. Hamburg Inn No. 2 is the only remaining location. Dave Panther, Fritz and Fran's son, bought the restaurant in 1979 from his parents and has continued the tradition of 'Comfort Food in a Fifties Time Capsule.' Dave Panther, *Burg Diner Liner,* July 2008

> Home Cooked Meals and Pastry Goods, Potato Salad, Baked Beans, Sandwiches, Lunches and Soft Drinks

Mrs. Van's menu, as mentioned in Bob Hibbs', *Iowa City,* 2001

The menu has remained surprisingly the same.

Fritz Panther is stocking behind the counter, Kathleen Carson on right, was a cook in the early 1950s

Steve Panther

Burg Memories

When Dad opened at 4 p.m. on Sunday, we would go to the early mass at St Mary's and then to the Burg. Among other things, the boys cleaned, peeled, cut, and blanched potatoes for French fries and rolled burger. We always fixed burgers for breakfast. Dill pickles on toast was a must.

We graduated to dish washing. In grades 7 and 8, I washed dishes before going to school. St. Mary's School was where the Catholic Student Center is now located. I returned to wash dishes after school.

Next step was serving tables. We wrote the orders on sheets of wax paper for the grill cooks. I received a tip 2 times in all of my serving time. The high-school-girl servers, especially if they were cute, would occasionally get a tip. Often we took the city bus home from work. We were saturated with the odor of burgers and fries.

Football days were huge. There were few restaurants in Iowa City and no fast food places like McDonald's. Dad set up an extra grill and French fryer in the back room to fill all of the to-go orders.

Working at the Burg was not optional. Dad said he grew up working on a farm, and the Burg was our farm.

"All of us had jobs to do when we were kids. It used to be that we didn't open on Sunday 'til 4 in the afternoon, so we'd clean up the place in the morning. And for a long time, we made the French fries for all the restaurants in the basement here. We'd cut and blanch 1,000 pounds of potatoes a week, 300-400 pounds at a time. After school, we'd go up and wash dishes or wait on tables." Then, as now, Hamburg Inn No. 2 had room for 32 diners at the 12-seat counter and in five booths. Thanks to a steady stream of customers from before dawn to near midnight, Dave says more than 300 guest checks are written every day. Staff Writer, *Cedar Rapids Gazette*, May 28, 1986

Arlene Ellis is at the cash register, early 1960s; Fran Panther picked out the changing wallpapers

Bill Panther

Here are some thoughts that I would like to share: #1. I remember that for $1.00 you could buy 2 hamburgers and a drink. (Amazing!) #2. Fritz worked @ the Burg all the time. Therefore, I got to really know my dad by working with him @ the Burg. #3. When I was in grade school, my responsibility was to make the French fries every morning before school and also, on the weekends for all three restaurants Burg #1, Burg #2, and Big Ten Inn. We would use several hundred pounds of potatoes on an Iowa Hawkeye football weekend. #4. My dad was very proud to put out a "good hamburger" and to receive compliments for the Burg food. #4. I feel working with my dad at the Burg gave me a good "work ethic." I also felt pride when the patrons would compliment the food, and I would feel bad when the food wasn't up to Burg standards.

Counter top—the first in a series of movie stills from a 1975 Super 8 film taken by Mary Bennett

Marty Panther

Dad had a lot of emotions tied up with the place. Nothing gave him more satisfaction than to get a compliment from a University of Iowa alumnus from the 50s or 60s, who had come in off I-80 and said they had spent a good part of their college days in the restaurant. They usually commented on seeing the coffee mugs made by Buffalo China that were there as far back as I can remember.

When the restaurant first opened, my dad's mom hung a crucifix by the steam tables to bless the place or to give it luck. Fritz had been brought up on a farm and was shaped by the Depression; that's where he got his work ethic. The family survived at the subsistence level in the 30s on his mom's vegetable garden, eggs, and canned chicken. Fritz delivered oil to farmers; he was up at 4:00 a.m. and never knew anything but work. During the first few weeks at the new restaurant he was very excited when he realized that business was good and he was his own boss.

Religion was always a big part of his life. He had gone to parochial school and sent his sons, too. He got the boys up at 5:00 a.m. on Sunday mornings for 6:00 Mass, followed by time in the restaurant repairing things or cleaning—Dad was a stickler for cleanliness. After a few hours, he took off the afternoon and had a nap. Periodically, the family went on a vacation, but Dad was never comfortable away from the restaurant. He thoroughly enjoyed working those hours. Only the occasional negative comment gave him a bad day.

He'd spent World War II on a merchant marine ship after attending Iowa Wesleyan College in Mt. Pleasant [on a track scholarship]. He went through Officer's Candidate School, emerged as a Lieutenant, and was assigned to a tanker—in charge of its gun crew. The gun crew shot down a few planes, although the ship was attacked several times and almost sunk by a torpedo.

After the war, Fritz went into partnership with his brother, Adrian, who enjoyed opening little restaurants in Cedar Rapids and Iowa City; they shared the work of grinding meat. But really, Fritz was content with his own niche at No. 2. The partnership in the Big 10 Inn was kind of a drag, especially when Riverside Drive was closed, causing a loss of business. Fritz was thrown into a depression, but one of his co-workers, a butcher named Otto, told him to "just come into work and do the best you can." "Put in a good day, one day at a time." The advice lifted him out of depression, as did the steady workers—housewives who were with him for 20-25 years: Annie, Lydia and Arlene come to mind. They liked him and felt that they were part of teamwork. Fritz was a good story-teller and also told a good joke; people liked his sense of humor. He was a good people person—someone that liked to hobnob.

Mom spent 99% of her time raising a family as a traditional housewife. She didn't even have a driver's license, but rode the bus and had

Cigarette display on top of pie case, circa 1979

her groceries delivered from the list she'd drawn up. Her contribution to the restaurant was making potato salad once a week. We could have pitched in more. We got off easy.

There's a picture of Dad that always stays with me. He's kneeling down, doing the books in the afternoon, a leg up next to the 24-pop bottle cases. In that state, he didn't hear you—you had to shake his shoulder; he was oblivious. He concentrated so hard, a bomb could go off.

Dave and Steve lived above the restaurant for a short time [Marty didn't]. The ventilation wasn't very good in those days so you could smell hamburgers and fries. Now I eat at the restaurant about once a month. For some reason, I always order a cheeseburger deluxe with either American fries or hash browns. It's also fun to bring guests and each order a different omelet; the Goosetown omelet is really good.   Personal communication

Wall menus— movie still

Mary Panther

Memories of Hamburg Inn (a few)

Mickey was a waitress that had worked at Hamburg Inn for many years. She once told Mike and Dave that she didn't think they realized how much she did for them and went on to relate that she got up every work day at, I believe, 3:30 a.m. to do her hair to look nice for them. Her appearance was clearly important to her from her perspective. She could be a bit intimidating. I remember once, eating at the counter for lunch, and Mickey was my waitress. After I had completed my meal, I asked her what kind of pie they had that day. She paused, leaned on the counter, and then took her order pad and whacked it on the counter in front of me. She looked at me, exasperated, and responded harshly, "I don't know what kind of pie we have!! I've been busy...." I quickly said that that was ok and that I didn't really need dessert anyway and left. That was just Mickey and she was a character in her own right.

There were many "unique" regulars that considered the place a second home of sorts. There was Clarence who came in daily at 5:30 a.m. He would order "the usual." This was eggs and sausage links, that he actually didn't eat, but had his own little dining ritual with. There was Barb, who would sit at the counter and chain smoke and drink her Diet Cokes for hours, through many afternoons, while her Mom held "card club" at home, after which she would return home, but not till she thought it was over. There were the Boch-y brothers who would collect the newspapers to use, we presumed, for fuel for their stove. Clearly they still must have been burning something, as they always came in with their clothes covered in some type of soot, and left the restaurant with a sample coating of soot on the sugar jar, salt and pepper shakers, or whatever else they'd touched. When one of the brothers died, the mortuary couldn't find the remaining brother the morning of his intended funeral, so they called the Burg, thinking he was likely there.

One thing that always struck me about the Hamburg Inn was Dave and Mike's generosity to people in general. I didn't work there until after Mike was killed, except on the rare occasion that he'd call me early on a Sunday morning when he needed to replace one of the student waitresses who didn't have a phone, overslept, or failed to show up for work for some reason. Of course, this was way before cell phones existed. I did work there with Dave though. And I was always greatly impressed and admiring of his kindnesses to both his employees and the customers. For years he has held a party for which he closes the restaurant and cooks and serves a meal for his employees and their entire families on New Years Eve. Dave has always been quiet and reserved but kind and fair to people from all walks of life. He was easy going to work with and allowed all the employees a lot of freedom and room for growth when they sought it. He expected only honesty and a fair work effort and respect for each other and the public.

Front counter— movie still

These are only a few vignettes of the many colorful people who have been "regulars" at the Hamburg Inn. I think what they all found there, what all of us found, who have found comfort there over the years, is that it has always been a warm and inviting place where anyone can feel at home and welcomed, regardless of your place in the world outside of the Burg.

From Mary: Mike and I were scheduled to be married privately with a JP, but he [Mike] was killed by a drunk driver a few weeks beforehand. He was my fiancé. I am a nurse by profession, but after his death I needed to take some time away from my career and chose to work at the restaurant... It was a way to kind of do what I saw as tying up some loose ends for Mike, sort of finishing some things, and to find comfort around others who also loved and missed him. I chose to take his name and changed my name legally as part of the process of dealing with a horrendous situation and it facilitated some healing for me as well.

Mike Panther in Halloween costume

Paris

Roma Panther

My Hamburg Inn Story

Although I didn't realize it, my Hamburg Inn story started in June, 1994. Dave Panther and I met for a cup of coffee (he doesn't even drink coffee but he sure dug into the pie) at a restaurant in Cedar Rapids. His "bio" from the dating service had said he was born and raised in Iowa City, he liked reading, traveling (this turned out to be a big plus!) and going to movies. David and I hit it off and began our courtship that year. Being from a small community northeast of Iowa City (Stanwood) little did I know that I was also falling for an owner of an "Iowa City icon," a storyteller, and "Babaloon" the clown. We married in 1996 and over the years by attending Food Shows, National Restaurant Shows and Restaurant Marketing seminars with Dave, I have honed my skills to be able to tell Hamburg Inn stories as if I had worked there all my life. And what a blessing it (and he!) has been!

Although the Panthers offer a varied menu, in 30 years I've never eaten anything but a cheeseburger, unless I stop in the morning for a cinnamon roll or late afternoon for pie a la mode....and coffee in one of those plain thick mugs that I think improves the taste. Iowa First Lady, Christie Vilsack, *Mt. Pleasant News*, April 1991

"My dad worked incredible hours," Dave said. "I tried to be my dad for a couple of years after I got into it but I didn't have the energy levels." Panther recalled the days before fast-food restaurants, when his dad would set up an extra grill in the back room to handle carry-out orders on weekends, especially during football season. Woodin, *Cedar Rapids Gazette,* September 1994

Original ad that ran on Wednesday, July 28, 1948, *ICPC*

"It's not fancy," [Dave] says of both the surroundings and the food that's served up there. "We're not trying to make a designer statement. We just serve good food at a reasonable price." The loyalty of Hamburg Inn fans is absolute. Panther points out that several of his better patrons eat there three meals a day every day of the week. Staff Writer, *Cedar Rapids Gazette,* May 28, 1986

Allan Gurganus

Local, Usual and Rare

Once upon a time at the Hamburg Inn Number Two (or was it Hamburg Inn Number One?) Breakfast cost you sixty-nine cents. We're talking 1974, and you got your two eggs any style, wheat toast paddled with butter, two pretty if chemical jellies, hash browns done 'al dente' and something called bottomless coffee. My great teachers at the Workshop were: John Cheever, Stanley Elkin, Stephen Becker, Jack Leggett, John Irving, and Miki, chief waitress at Hamburg Inn Number Two, or was it Number One. [?] Such are the caprices of memory.

I'd arrived from a semi-self-congratulatory school in the Northeast and, at twenty-three, was sophisticated as only an undergraduate in commuting distance of Manhattan weekends can be. Basted in Dickens, Chekhov, James and Proust, my idea of fiction hovered somewhere between Europe and the nineteenth century, my own morbid sensitivity and a Bloomsbury dream of perfect company that'd be as intellectually erotic, that'd say funny things, that would have just enough money not to mention it, a crowd that would enjoy frequent sex and even more frequent publication and—of course—look good.

    Then the plane landed amongst corn, more of it than seemed either possible or necessary. I arrived overdressed. Some things never change.

    I'd been told that the Middle West grew persons doughy, deacon-like, devoid of eccentricity, slaves to duty. In Iowa City, the cab passed a service station, its fore yard planted with huge sunflowers and, again, corn, stalks eight feet high. Was this a joke, a pun? I didn't understand. Arriving at my Victorian boarding house, I opened the bathroom door, I noticed a handsome young woman seated on the commode. She said quite plainly, "We share. I don't know you. But, I'm here just now."

    I said, "Hi," closed the door and fell against a wall.

    Sharing bathrooms with strangers—very un-Bloomsbury.

All I'll say about the Seventies being the Seventies is that they came between the Sixties, which you've heard too much about, the Eighties which, for better or worse, we're in—so in—and that whatever we did during the Seventies, we probably would've done—in different hairstyles and bellbottoms—in other decades, using different reasons to explain ourselves. Or maybe I just think that because the Seventies were, like—so . . . Seventies, right? But let that go.

    Porn movies were being shot in my boarding house's front apartment. Hogging the bathroom, trim young people applied body make-up from gallon jugs. I hoped to be asked over, if only as a consultant. I was not. I found our white bathroom specked with flesh-colored droplets. My education cranked up. My conception of the Middle West began to thaw.

On Iowa Avenue, an old man walked his young cat on a leash. But the cat went everywhere cats do—under fences, beneath cars—and you soon saw: a young cat out walking its old man.

My fellow students looked wild and ready—but decent compared to how the town was acting up. I sensed there was more English and Philosophy jostling on the streets than in a building named for E. and P.

And then I met Miki. A type-A waitress, short, Mason-jar shaped, gloomy, brilliantly efficient, semi-mean. I'd seen her make younger, fellow serving persons weep behind the coffee tanks. Miki wore hushpuppy shoes stained nurse-white against their will, she had wing glasses and, under a double-hairnet, pin-curls even then long out-of-date. She carried twelve (count them) steaming coffee mugs contorted around the usual ten fingers. Not at gunpoint would Miki call anybody "Sugar."

I settled—dressed down now—on a counter stool, I ordered the same breakfast three days running. Morning four, it happened, over the heads of others fueling up for work, Miki called to me, "The usual?" I nodded, hard. "Usual, Mik." (I was, as my grandmother might say, "entering in.")

True, a week later, eating the usual, I had un-monogamous thoughts about French toast—but I stuck with my standard fare. Otherwise, the usual would *not* be.

This was to become a great discovery. It's hard to explain how the bullying reigning waitress provided an algebra I needed. I began wondering about Miki—whose last name I never knew. When she dreamed, if she dreamed—did she dream about fishing, about waitressing in a better place, growing strawberries, did she dream she was the mother of three, headed home to cook supper? What was Miki's hidden poem? The more unlike me she seemed, the more I needed her news. I could not dismiss her. Can you name one rounded sympathetic working-person in the novels of Virginia Woolf? I'd arrived with some elitist notion of separation between artist and subject matter. Now I found Us and Them becoming uncomfortably synonymous.

At local thriftshops, I perfected my Iowa disguise. I got a battered green Schwinn and—with a story freshly finished—I'd pedal it to a friend's place. While he read me indoors, I paced the porch like an expectant father. And friends rushed their fiction to me. We were entranced with each other. We were our own news. Talking shop about Kafka, we ate truckstop breakfasts late at night. We took certain drugs, we fell in love with each other and out again and ended up with broken hearts but my God what subject matter.

Meantime, weekly, on the Workshop's worksheet, Iowa City itself always presented the best poem or story:

A vague young woman from my boarding house explained: She lived here to be around the school's symphony conductor—a man she'd never said one word to, not aloud. She didn't *need* to. She attended all his rehearsals. She hid at the back of Hancher Auditorium—picking up the conductor's every in-joke, all his loving thoughts beamed her way—via transistors cleverly implanted in her molars. "We all have a mission here," she smiled. I nodded. I began to believe her.

"The usual?" Miki called as I brushed snow from my hair. It was already January. (Such hair I had then, and cascading down to here.) "Usual," said I, imagining all the menus banqueting in her head, forty years' worth. Maybe even Flannery O'Connor's yen for a mornings's dry toast, served eucharist-plain, with a large side of tabasco. (I just made that up.)

The coffee mug clomped before me, not a drop spilled as Miki, oracle, went, "Guess you heard."

Miki was like Time itself: An express making only local stops.

"No," I said. "Haven't . . . heard." You *had* to say that to get the stuff out of her. First you admitted not being from around here, then—an artist having humbled you, Miki—as folks will—told:

"Not heard? Seems—man down to Aetna Realty. Working late. Stepped in the elevator. Nothing there. Fell clear down the shaft. Busted both legs . . . compound. Lay in the grease and gunk for nine full hours. Janitor heard the screaming. Man's a regular. Always sits there, not two stools from *your* favorite. He's American cheese omelette. He's hold the fries. He's hot tea, plenty of lemon on the side. He's danish. Not much of a tipper, short-fused fellow. Still . . . wouldn't wish that on somebody else's dog."

A night watchman, just off duty at the gas plant, slumped onto the stool beside mine. "Usual, George? Guess you heard. No? Where *you* been? Man down to Aetna Realty. Working late. Stepped in the elevator. Nothing there. Fell clear . . ."

Then—happy to be sitting among other non-Bloomsbury workers— (me, headed to my little Hermes portable—*Some*body had to do it)— an idea opened like the morning's first sweet caffeine: Chekhov had taught me back East, Workshop classes showed me and now Miki reiterated, but she did it best: "The usual" isn't really.

"The usual"—two words—must mean something different for every customer.

It was definitely snowing outside Hamburg Inn Number One or Two. I felt weightless with the heaviness of my own discovery. I was really young then. We all were.

Like everybody, I believed I was the first.

Returning in 1986, I planned to walk to every house I'd ever rented (or—thanks to love affairs, however brief—spent even one night in). And I did. Which is why I came a day and a half early.

I had a Miki fantasy: I would step in after twelve years' absence. She'd frown at me over today's young customers. Then something would unlatch behind her glasses and, over other workers' heads, over a dozen years, she says, "The usual?" I nod. Like nodding to the world. Very un-Bloomsbury, nodding greedily to the word "usual."

The new waitress told me. Miki died last year—died after falling down behind her counter here while serving others omelettes and dark news. For awhile there, about her, strangers on these stools must've muttered to each other, "I guess you heard . . . Miki."

"Work-shop"—a shop where work is done.

I was a worker, in thrift-store coveralls, planted at her counter among other laborers—no better or worse than me—all of us lined there in a row like . . . corn or something. I loved Iowa City then. It and my writing were the same things. I loved my friends and their work, equally. I loved being so young and having so far to go and believing I could manage it.

For me the, "Meltdown" might've meant some Hamburg Inn blue-plate special. Reagan was a toothless has-been B actor. AIDS, you took for indigestion. I am lucky, still alive. We all know how many aren't. Those of us left, we're still trying, aren't we?

Once we wanted to get into this school, and we did.

Now we wanted to come back here, and we have.

We are the lucky ones—despite all our whining about grants and jobs and who got what. Writing is still manual labor. We must take our cue from Miki: we're in it, not just for the tips—but for the job's sake. Here we are now—a Bloomsbury of the Prairie—only better. I glance around. We look okay. And yet, I ask myself, if *we're* doing fairly well—then why is the world such a mess? How do we get the two better lined up—us, its chroniclers—and it, our breakfast bread-and-butter?

To the workers in our field, still waiting to learn to breathe then speak then sing—I'd say, when in doubt about subject matter, common geography, a place to start—begin with "Right here." The truth is always local first—and then, if true enough, it spreads. Settle in a room and read to one another. Read talkingly and—afterwards—about the poem or story—talk readingly.

Okay, change from mimeo to Xerox. But keep it real untechnological. Keep the simple, ordinary and decent there at your workshop table's very very center. Maybe that will save us.

Miki? I think we're ready to order. You—total memory of menus—you, newsworthy in the Iowa Ballroom tonight —we don't ask for eternity. But we've had fifty years of something good here.

So, could you, please, bring us fifty more of the same, please?

Of, yes,

The usual.

Alan Gurganus attended and taught at the Writers Workshop; he is a nationally revered writer of novels and short stories. "'Local, Usual and Rare." is reprinted from *The Iowa Review*, Vol 19, No 1 (1989)

One of the individual record selectors at each booth— movie still

Francis/Fritz and Frances Panther in the back room—in what is now the grill; 1950s

Aprons were part of the early 1960s uniform; Dave Ellis is in back

MRS. VAN'S CAFE
HOME COOKED MEALS

A Little History

The Hamburg Inn is in its 64th year of serving tasty meals, but the building itself dates from the late 19th century. According to Dave, it was a water company and then a meat market. City directories show Julius and Hendrie Heintz were running a meat market at the Linn Street address in 1926, but others may have pre-dated them. Meats were smoked on the premises and hung in the front room from one of the hooks in the ceiling, found during the restoration. According to Beverly Dolezal, Lucas Vander Linden, her grandfather, was operating Van's meat market by 1938, probably earlier. The Vander Linden family had originated in Pella and Lucas was known for his "Genuine German bologna." The meat was smoked in a small shed behind the restaurant, turned into sausage rings, and sold at the market and later at his wife's restaurant.

Sometime in the next two years, the stylish metamorphosis from butcher shop to restaurant occurred under his wife, Mrs. Nona C. Vander Linden. The creamy light walls and simple, uncluttered space make Mrs. Van's Cafe look like an inviting stop for a hot meal or a slice of homemade pie. Nona Rucker was born in 1896 in Mountain Grove, Missouri. She was strong and independent and though not highly educated was able to support herself and thrive during difficult times. Her granddaughter remembered her as warm-hearted and always willing to help others. When her temper erupted it was with "frustration at things, not at people." She liked making home-cooked meals on the Roper stove in the kitchen of the cafe rather than working as a grill cook, though she employed University students as short order cooks and servers—before some of them went into service. During the war years, if a soldier was in uniform, he was not charged for a meal.

The menu board in one photo lists:

        cheese sandwiches, 10¢ toasted, 15¢
        fried egg, 10¢
        peanut butter, 10¢
        hot beef & pork, 20¢
        cold ham, 15¢ fried, 20¢
        cheeseburger, 20¢

Beverly remembers the aroma of the bolongna rings and of her grandmother's hot roast beef special with mashed potatoes, gravy, a vegetable, bread, butter and dessert—probably a slice of pie with a scoop of vanilla ice cream from Hutchinson's dairy store on the corner of Gilbert and Market. Coffee was served in heavy white mugs, similar to the ones used today. Carbonated drinks were advertised in the front window; there were: Graf's, from the bottling works next door, So-Grape, or Cleo's Cola. The cafe operated from 6:30 a.m. until 8:00 p.m. At that time, one entered the cafe on the alley side of the building and sat in one of the front booths or at the

Mrs. Nona Vander Linden with her grandchildren: Archie and Beverly, circa 1939

Left: Mrs. Van's daughter, Frances Treptow, holding her daughter, Beverly and dog, Tippy, in front of what was probably Van's Meat Market, circa spring 1937—Old Homestead hams are on sale; right: Mrs. Van with her aunt, Della Canaday, 1944, with reflection of buildings across Linn St. in window.

Beverly before a Mrs. Van's Cafe window display for Graf's Soda, circa 1938

Student employees before Mrs. Van's, circa 1944—the fate of these men and other employees who went into service is not known.

counter in back. Pies were arrayed in a window pie-case along with a lavish display of Mrs. Van's plants. For years, Beverly was her only grandchild and she said Nona was a soft touch and could be relied on for a dime to go to the movie or to get a treat. Nona and Lucas lived above the cafe and after the lunch crowd had come through, she would head upstairs for an afternoon nap. By 1948, she was tired enough to give up the business and try something new. She bought a home at 918 Newton Street and rented Mrs. Van's Rooms to hospital visitors. In later life, she remarried to Dee Walker of Las Cruces, New Mexico; she died in 1966 and is buried in Memory Gardens under the Vander Linden name. Her vision of a restaurant on the near northside led to the Panther's choice of 214 Linn Street in 1948.

This ad appeared in the 1940 Iowa City Directory, but was updated from its original use as a Reich's Chocolate Shop ad in the early 30s.

Right: It's 12:53 on the clock and the calendar reads 1944; cake and ice cream are being served at Beverly's 10th Birthday Party by family friend, Jenny Griffith, on left and Mrs. Van; Aunt Ina Lefers, Marilyn Luse Laschke, a friend, and Beverly Treptow Dolezal are seated at the counter; note the booths behind her, the two doors that lead to the back kitchen, and those familiar white mugs on the back shelves.

Nona's Birthday Party, circa 1938, in the kitchen of what is now the Hamburg Inn; she is surrounded by kitchen help—back row: unknown man, Mr. Treeboken, unknown man—holding what looks like a photo of this room, Mr. Lockwood, Harold DeReus, Justin Furstenberg; front row: Lucas Vander Linden, Shorty, Mrs. Nona Vander Linden, Wnona De Reus, her daughter, and Beverly Dolezal

The 1928 Iowa City Directory states that the tiny white building owned by Ralph W. Wharton at 119 E. Iowa Avenue was named the

Hamburg Inn.
Whether for economic reasons, fatigue or the wish to try something new, Mr. Wharton turned the restaurant over as a rental to Joseph A. Panther of Mt. Pleasant, Iowa, between 1935-1936 (city directories were printed in alternate years). Joe carried on the Hamburg Inn name but never moved to Iowa City, although his younger brother Adrian did, to attend college and to manage the restaurant. Eventually Adrian purchased the cement block building—it was not as stylish as Mrs. Van's, but is there today behind the facade of Joe's Place.

The Panther's were familiar with the restaurant business through Frances Fitzpatrick, the wife of third brother, Fritz Panther (the couple owned Hamburg Inn No. 2). Her brother, Ty Fitzpatrick, ran Ty's Grill in Mt. Pleasant, where in the 1950s, Dave remembered that fountain cokes were still mixed from gallon-jug concentrates. Fran's cousin, Cornelius "Connie" Hurley, managed the Big Ten Inn in Iowa City for the Panthers, a dinner restaurant with a drive-in and car-hop.

Dave estimates that over the years, he and his father have hired more than 1,000 employees at the Burg. The dress code for the waitstaff, mostly female in the beginning, was nice looking street clothes and an apron for the women, white shirt and dark pants for the men—no jeans. Jeans are still discouraged today but the familiar T-shirts with the logo have been added, as well as lots of personal adornments. Dave said they try to strike a balance.

In the beginning, local women made the soups and baked the pies for Fritz' No. 2 restaurant, until pie delivery became too inconsistent, so they went to premade pies (those from the Farmer's Market make an appearance in season). Asked if business has been simplified or not over the years—they no longer peel 1,000 pounds of potatoes a week—Dave said, "both." "Dad didn't know an omelette. He had a simpler menu. The biggest item was the special." Today the cooks prepare soups, chili, and cakes from scratch and are beginning to implement a change to more in-house items.

When asked if he is tired, he said "all the time." Although compared to his dad's work load of 6 1/2 days a week and no manager, Dave lately puts in an easier 2 1/2 day week and takes the occasional trip because of his capable management team. His personal food favorites are a burger and grilled onions for breakfast and a tenderloin or chili for lunch. These also reflect the most popular choices on the menu: burgers and tenderloins. Most of the meat is raised in Iowa (none from beyond the Midwest) and burgers now weigh 6 oz.

While he missed the Reagan visit, Dave did get to meet President Clinton—the first visit was a surprise stop—and he remarked on how personable, how charismatic Clinton was. He was easy to talk to and could engage anyone. Clinton remembered to sit in the same place on his next visit. Candidate Barack Obama chose to stand and greet people and staff in the diner. Dave also said that Joe Biden was impressive in person.

Marybeth Slonneger

I was there in 73-74. I was 18-19 years old. I worked part-time and mostly Friday/Saturday evenings 5-2am! I always remember wanting the door locked just before 2am so that the after-bar crowd would not be too many. I was trained to cook and I remember Fritz showing me how to form the burger and cook on the grill. We would line up buns on the wood board in front of the grill and prep each burger, left to right, according to the order. There were mini juke boxes attached to the wall at each booth and you flipped pages to select your songs. There was one pinball machine located in the front corner. Before and while working there, I spent many nights playing pinball and munching fries at Hamburg Inn. David L. Keeley, personal correspondence

Long-time cook, Kathleen Carson, turning burgers on the griddle;
she later became the manager of the Airport Inn

He [Dave] had two fantasies about the restaurant when he was growing up. One was that it was the "last place I ever wanted to be. The other was the fantasy of owning it." First Lady, Christie Vilsack, *Mt. Pleasant News*, April 1991

The 1980s round-counter look, until remodeling in 1990

Cinda Kornblum

Late Night at the Hamburg Inn

"A little bit of choice makes a color regular. A little bit of black makes dinner necessary." --Gertrude Stein

A new blue notebook can make anyone a poet,
but an old dusty Greyhound
whisking a lover into the black of night
sends one immediately to the Hamburg Inn
where I sit now
watching the door expectantly.

There were once those who knew the sun
knew the stars, knew all the answers.
If only one of them would walk in
I would recognize him instantly
and could invite him over
for tea or sake or coffee or mead

Oh, the many futures that comes to mind.
Time to watch them all at the Hamburg Inn.

Setting: Alone at the Hamburg Inn
Time of day: Early evening
Who's involved: A young man, smiling, with dark eyes

Description: He walks in, sits down & we converse easily & intimately. I begin:

The No. 2 logo on the window was designed by Dave, who based it on train engine numbering.

"I have always had a strange fascination
      with vacuum cleaners
and monsters that look like vacuum cleaners
      and women who ride vacuum cleaners
      cleaning ashes
      from their loved ones' pipes."

      "My fantasies have many alternate endings,"
      he says, adding salt to his tenderloin, then continues,
      "I have dreamed of giving bras to the wind and:
      --watching the wind parade through town proudly encased, or
--of the wind violently ripping the bra from its breast to run naked again through the trees or
--of the wind growing old and sagging until the bra no longer
supports the breast
but drops
      to its knees
            to catch it
                  lovingly."

But someone has burst through the Hamburg Inn door screaming,
"Is the grill fired up? Is the grill fired up?
I wanna know is the grill fired up?"
"That guy's really drunk," I say routinely to the next table
then revert back to my silence.

In my daydreams,
I pose questions to myself
and answer them in many possible ways
rehearsing the lines knowing that
when the situation comes up in reality
I do not know what I'll say
till I hear my voice speak the words.
If only I knew what state I'd be in

or who I'd be with or how old…
Plans can be made but the time can only be right
when you've almost forgotten about it.

I look at the clock.
The restaurant echoes with the sounds of
now-retired cooks cursing
over the hot grill
as one table rates the food
and another table rates a movie.

Suddenly my friend is back & we burst into rhyme-verging-on-song:

>Rated R for revolting
>Rated P for patronizing
>Rated X for extra dollar to get in
>
>Rated R for racy dialogue
>Rated P for practically boring
>Rated G for goddamn kids make too much noise
>
>Rated S for sappy sentiments
>Rated N for normal sex scenes
>Rated B for blood & guts in living color…

The other customers gladly pick up the song & we sit back
knowing that the waitress will soon fill our coffee
and ask for a nickel apiece.

The sun is hot
The sun is really hot
but it's not just the heat, it's vinyl heat!
The heat of the vinyl reminding me that nothing is real,

as the waitress makes me say I want cream
before she gives it to me
AND IT'S NOT EVEN CREAM!
I WANT MY MONEY BACK.
YOU SAID THIS WAS CREAM.
I scream it at the top of my lungs
and the plaster on the ceiling starts to crumble.
The cracks form letters, then words—
It is a message!
I am suddenly a member of this odd group at the Hamburg Inn.
"You are the chosen ones," the plaster says
and I wake up instantly.
THIS IS NOT ONE OF THE FUTURES THAT IS POSSIBLE.

A pause, if it lasts long enough
will always draw one's attention toward the clock.
Just time's way of inflating its own importance.
Many times I've sat here
with the clock looking at me
surprised as I am now
pulling on my coat
debating (or not debating)
about a tip for the waitress—
the waitress who I will remember
not as an employee
but as the restaurant itself.
Just as the waitress is employed
so am I and it is time to go.

It is time to go and I cannot go yet. This is the time when everything comes back to me I had so much to say and I wanted the evening to continue I am on my feet now and near the door and I don't want to go so I linger forever.

Hamburg Inn #1, 1970-1972, Reprinted from *The Actualist Anthology*

Cinda and Allan Kornblum were regulars at Hamburg Inn #1 in the early 1970s. Allan published *Toothpaste*, a mimeographed poetry magazine, which grew into Toothpaste Press and later Coffee House Press now located in Minneapolis. In those days Iowa City was energized with poetry on the streets and Coralville was just a strip where the Skelly Diner could be found open at all hours. The Toothpaste Press archives are preserved in the University of Iowa Special Collections.

Late Night at the Hamburg Inn

A collaborative poem between Cinda Kornblum, who wrote the words, and Dave Morice, who did the drawing, 1970s

Lucy Ordin, early 1950s

Pauline Hamm was my mom's sister and she moved to Iowa City after her husband Gene died. She worked at Big 10 Inn until it closed in the 70s and then started working at Hamburg Inn. Pauline was a Great help to my dad and mom and eventually to me in putting that personal family touch to the everyday running of "The Burg." Dave Panther

Waitress Pauline Hamm is talking to Joe Connell on the left, 1970s

After working at the restaurant nearly 40 years, waitress Pat Hinkel, 62, knows customers' names, keeps their coffee cups filled and often knows their orders when they step in the door.... "I'm the last one of the old ones. The rest of the housewives moved on or passed away..." She started at the Hamburg the autumn after her high school graduation in 1955 after seeing an ad in the paper.... "I like coming in and seeing the regular faces," she said. Shim, *Iowa City Press-Citizen,* March 1999

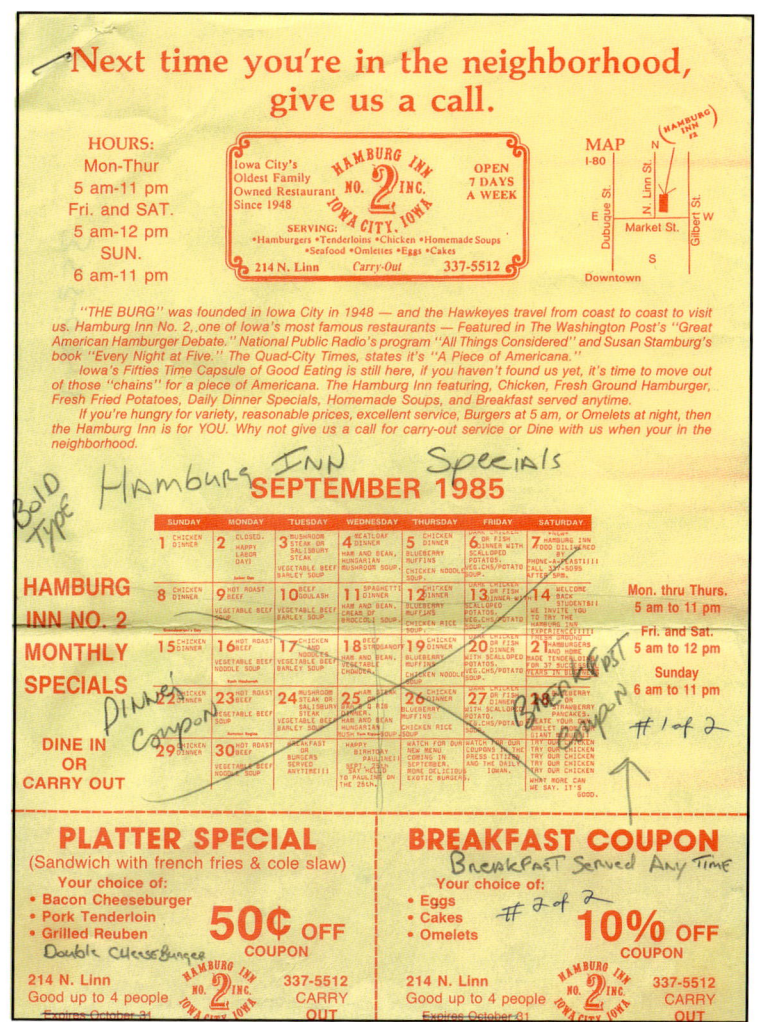

It doesn't look like much, but it's filled with lots of pleasant surprises. What a nice change from other establishments in this town who do but aren't. Henry Olson, *The Daily Iowan*, ND

James Alan McPherson

Several months ago my daughter, Rachel, sent me from Barcelona, Spain, a street map she had drawn of Iowa City. She had recollected from her deep experiences in this community some loving images. She had drawn an arrow from our home at 711 Rundell Street, through downtown Iowa City, stopping at our favorite video-rental store, then on to the Simmons home on River Street [family friends], then back downtown to Hamburg Inn on Linn Street. I was amazed at Rachel's vivid memories of Iowa City, since she had not grown up here and only has memories printed on her recollections from her many visits here. Although Ellie Simmons is dead and the video store has been displaced by Netflix, Rachel's memories of our vital places in Iowa City are still alive, even in competition with the deeply historic and romantic images of ancient Spain. I framed this street map and set it on a special shelf, and for many months I brooded why these specific images could capture and keep vital Rachel's best memories of Iowa City.

These days, when I am mostly housebound with diabetes and unable to walk or drive without difficulty, I depend on a "Caring Hands" service for housework and for my meals. Although the caretakers are excellent helpers, I still catch myself recalling when I was able to walk freely about Iowa City, and when I used to know the places where I could truly enjoy my meals. I do not mean here to downsize lunches from McDonald's or Burger King's, but sometimes I do recollect, with a taste of delicious flavors, the lunches and dinners I used to enjoy in a specific restaurant. In Cambridge, there was Mr. Bartlett's Burger Cottage on Massachusetts Avenue, just across from Harvard Yard. Back during the middle l960s, I lived in an apartment which I earned working as a janitor in a building at 8 Plympton Street, a structure which encased Mr. Bartlett's on its ground floor. Each day, from early morning until late evening, I could smell inside my apartment the flavorsome meals being prepared down in Mr. Bartlett's. I very, very often walked downstairs to claim my share. Then, during the late l960s, when I was a student in the Writers Workshop, I lived in an apartment called Black's Gaslight Village at 422 Brown Street, just a few blocks away from the Burg. There, as during my Mr. Bartlett days in Cambridge, I would enjoy the very warm company of increasingly familiar patrons who shared a comparable, unending taste for the meals they served.

I have always considered Hamburg Inn as a personal "friend" within the community. In more recent years Hamburg Inn has not changed that much. It still affirms through delectable handshakes its affinity for its neighbors. It still serves the very same mouth-watering and deliciously crisp meals to the very same set of clients—oldtimers,. students, and newcomers to Iowa City. But what has changed is the world outside its doors. Chain restaurants and chain grocery stores have all but displaced community grocers like our own 'Johns' on the corner of Muscatine and Court in our neighborhood. The communal bond I shared with the owner for many, many years caused him to tell me that the Hy-Vee chain store down Muscatine desired John's meat customers and had filed a complaint with city agencies alleging that the refrigeration used by John's was obsolete and needed to be replaced. Since the owner could not

Brittany serving guests

afford the replacement, the independent grocery store was forced to shut its doors on its neighbors in this old area of Iowa City.

I imagine that the very same thing is happening to small businesses all over the country. Corporate retailers are displacing small businesses that were once firmly grounded in their communal landscapes. Parents passed on to children their communal names. People carried these stores in their memories, and most especially in their emotions, the faces of friends. Perhaps I am ignoring the economic savings conferred by corporate businesses on their customers. I admit that I am biased here. Since my ideal model of a communal business is based on those like Mr. Barlett's Burger Cottage and Hamburg Inn, I desire them to keep on displaying the warm, somewhat emotional, personal interactions that one would expect from a good neighbor. Instead of corporate efficiency, one might expect delightful "stalls" in efficiency grounded in personal interactions with familiar clients. This is the degree of personal "neighboring" that I have always encountered inside Hamburg Inn.

Is it a fantasy to expect a business to take on the emotional traits of a "person?" Just now we are seeing in the media a rising outcry against corporate business practices and their "unmannered" outreach into American domestic life. Protesters seem to demand that corporations behave more like human beings, that they display more human manners. This demand may seem fantasy-based and unrealistic until one considers the origins of the corporate birth. As a black American, a descendent of slaves, I trace my "legal" American roots back to the 13th, 14th, and 15th Amendments to the U.S. Constitution. The 13th freed the slaves. The 14th conferred U.S. citizenship. And the 15th gave the slaves the right to vote. What is most often overlooked is that the "permanent national citizenship" created by the 14th amendment later became the basis of corporate identity, one loosened from restrictions placed on them by individual states. "All persons born or naturalized in the United States are citizens of the United States and of the states wherein they reside…" While the tradition of "paramount national citizenship" took hold for corporate "persons" during the years following the Civil War, it only began to take hold for black Americans during the Civil Rights Movement.

Of course it seems quite foolish now to consider a multinational corporation as a "person." Still, it is not so foolish to consider a friendly mom and pop store or another business like Hamburg Inn as a "person." One has to admit that some businesses, especially the smaller ones, exude friendly personalities. The food prices notwithstanding, the character traits extended by the people within them, and most especially, the care they give to their customer-friends remind one that one is not merely having a meal but enjoying it with members of a caring family. The clues reside within the casual and warm hands of the waitresses and waiters, their smiles, their impulses ("Is the food seasoned to your taste?") Even your stinginess in tipping them seems not to be personally offensive. Like family members, they will forgive your bad manners and treat you with genuine warmth the next time you sit at their tables. All of those personal habits, and countless others, are present in the daily behavior of the people serving in Hamburg Inn. The behavior of the serving staff defines the "character" or the "personality" of the enterprise. They embody the archetype behind the stereotype "home cooking" and "caring hands." The more like "home" a place feels, the more it is considered a neighbor or a friend.

I feel this way about the Hamburg Inn. During all my years in Iowa City, this small restaurant has been my constant friend, cultivating me through all my solitary meals. I truly cannot remember or imagine, much like Rachel, my daughter, Iowa City without it.

James Alan McPherson is an American short story writer and essayist. He has been a recipient of a Guggenheim Fellowship, a MacArthur Fellowship and the first Paul Engle Award conferred by the University of Iowa. He is a member of the permanent faculty of the Iowa Writers' Workshop.

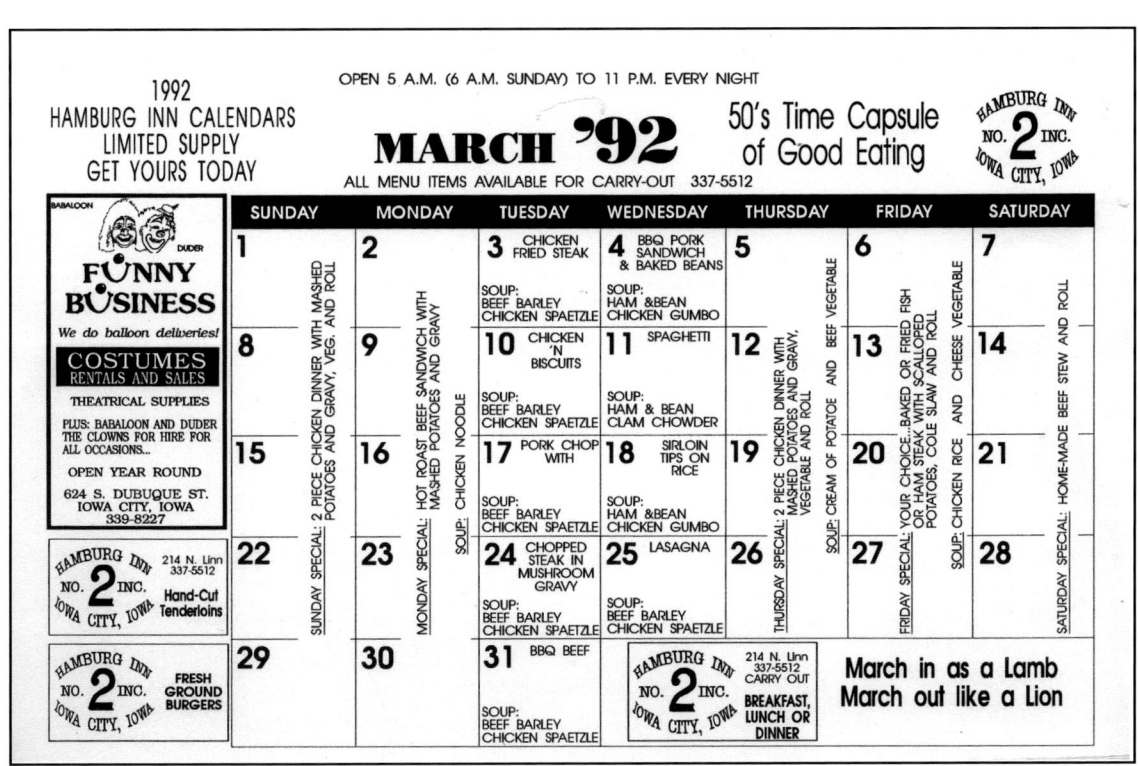

Mary (Stroh) Swanson

Iowa City Literary Insanity

You've been trying all night
and she just won't come.
The bottle is empty, the page
is blank. Your Muse...
where is she?
In the heavy stirring
of an Iowa August sun, you feel her.
She's leaning on your shoulder.
One strand of her hair
gets twisted around your fingertip.
Her presence, and the pink dawn
lift you from your chair. Together
you walk through the echoing streets.
It's your Muse's arm around you,
her soft talking that makes you smile.
She whispers, "You are brilliant!"
As the merchants unroll their awnings,
sweep their walkways... you're convinced:
Everything Has Meaning!
By the time you get to the Hamburg Inn
you're brushing tears from your eyes,
gratefully. Though it's difficult to speak,
you order coffee for yourself
and your invisible Muse.
The waitress brings two cups.
Why not? She's seen it all before.

Case for homemade pies— movie still

I first got to Iowa City in 1971. I was a single mom with a one year old daughter. Hamburg Inn #1, on Iowa Avenue, was the place we'd go for a hot meal and a game on the pinball machine. It was different than all the places where the college kids hung out. It had the feel of a workingman's diner. I felt comfortable bringing my child with me and talking with the people I met there.

I eventually went back to school at U of I. I was accepted into the undergrad Writer's Workshop and began publishing a small press literary magazine (*Me Too*) with Patricia Markert. Hamburg Inn was the site of many, many hours spent discussing poetry, politics and publications. I can still remember the feeling of walking through the freezing cold and opening the door to the steamy warmth of the Hamburg Inn. I can still remember the long hours on a lazy summer afternoon of intense conversations, of kids climbing around the booths, of some decent food even though I had little money. I can still remember the sense of belonging. It was a safe haven for me and I can't imagine Iowa City without it.

Mary Swanson currently divides her time between San Francisco, CA and Middlebury, VT as she continues her 20 year practice as a Medical Intuitive. She has two daughters and a brilliant grandson. Of her time in Iowa City, from 1971 to 1980, she says, "It was a time of intense transformation for me. I learned I had something to offer. I learned to respect myself." She continues to write poetry and is currently learning to paint portraits in oil. If you'd like to know more about her, go to maryswanson.net.

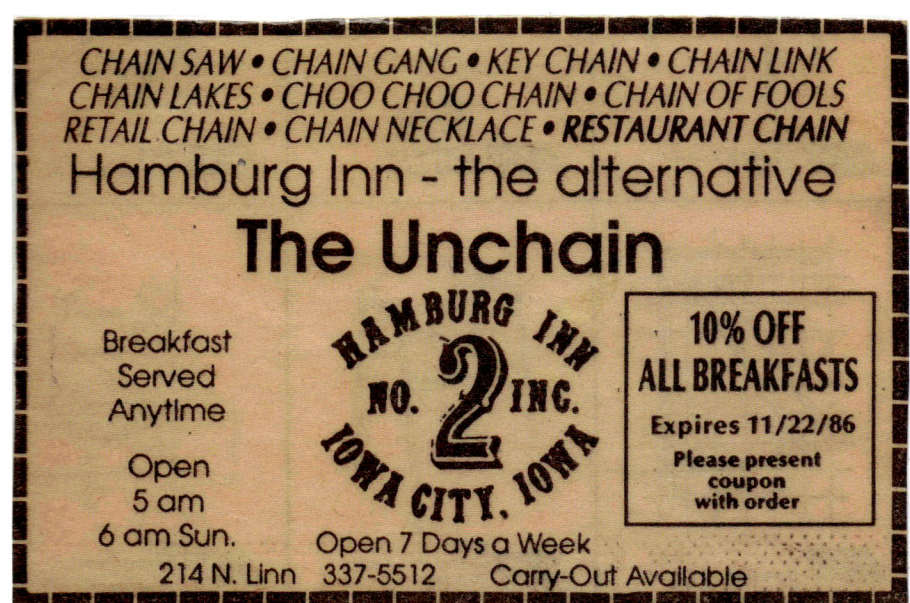

Playing the pinball machine— movie still

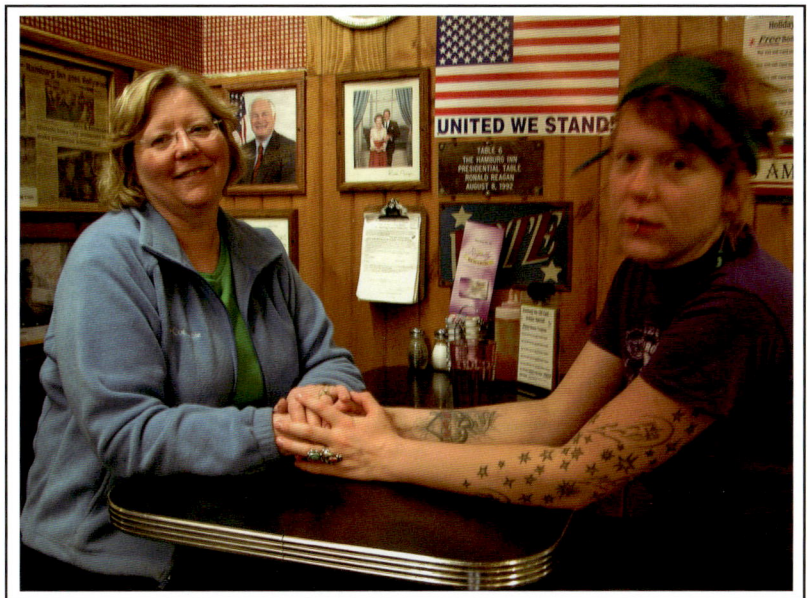

Emily talking to her mom after her night shift

When [Joe] Panther hired his first waitress in 1938, she was paid $6 a week, plus a meal. At the close [of Hamburg Inn #1], waiters and waitresses were paid $2.75 an hour... Heth, *Des Moines Register,* May 1978

Saturday, August 10, 1973, *Iowa City Press-Citizen*

Ronald Reagan once dug into a $4.25 daily lunch special and now has the Presidential booth named after him. Fruehling, July 1999

Table 6 for the President

Table 6 has been dubbed the *Hamburg Inn Presidential Table* though two Democratic presidents chose to sit elsewhere. But Reagan did initiate presidental stops here. Table 6 can be seen opposite, under the framed photograph of President and Mrs. Reagan that was given to the restaurant. Unfortunately, staff didn't think to take a picture of Reagan on the day of his visit.

This was the only place he [President Ronald Reagan] ate in Iowa City... He spoke at the Hoover Library giving the re-dedication speech, and afterward he came here to eat lunch. That was on August 8, 1992. [Manager Dave] Cohen says that Reagan's secret service personnel had called the restaurant a few days earlier to warn the management that there was a chance that he might be stopping there. They also asked about the special that day. "We don't generally run a special on Saturdays," Cohen says. "However, they did tell us that he really likes meat loaf. So we made meat loaf our special that Saturday." Risch, *The Hawk's Eye*, Summer 1994

"I remember serving Reagan, just like he was one of the guys," Cohen says. "We have great Dutch apple pie. He asked for that first, before his meal. He wanted a scoop of vanilla ice cream on his pie, too. After the dessert he settled for our special of the day. It was meat loaf and he really cleaned his plate." Wundram, *Quad-City Times*, September 1993

Mary Helen Stefaniak

The Burg and I

My relationship with the Hamburg Inn began before I ever set foot in the place. I was back in Milwaukee with the kids when my husband set out, a one-man scouting party, to find in Iowa City 1) a job, and 2) just the right counter-service restaurant to replace the breakfast-and-burger joint that had served as my office in Milwaukee. He was successful on both counts. I can still remember how happy he sounded when he called me to report that he'd spent a couple of precious dollars on a hamburger and coffee at this place called Hamburg Inn No. 2. It had a counter and booths, he said, and there were people reading and writing all over the place, especially at the counter. Also, the food was good, and the waitress had refilled his coffee cup before he thought to ask.

All I had to report was that my mother still couldn't believe we were taking her grandchildren to Idaho.

It was 1982. In those days, the daytime waitresses tended to be women of a certain age. There was Micky, who was famous for remembering the "usual" of all her regulars even long after they'd finished school and left town; and Millie, who inspired so much loyalty and affection in two of her regulars—my friend Nancy Loeb and me—that when we heard she'd had a heart attack, we visited her in the ICU. We attempted to serve her a glass of ice water, but, lacking waitress skills of our own, we spilled it all over her instead. The monitors went wild.

The way I remember it, Dave and Mike Panther were always on hand, brothers and heirs to the kingdom. Mike was taller, broader of shoulder, louder of laugh; Dave was the quieter of the two, his inner clown waiting to emerge. Among our favorite waiters were Gary, your friendly lunch time waiter, politico, and public access TV personality; Steve, greeter of Presidents past, future, and sitting (along with a succession of Iowa primary hopefuls); and Paul, the one who changed his name to Gabriel and made himself a very convincing waitress for Halloween.

Paul/Gabriel freaked my mother out one time, while she was visiting from Milwaukee. She and Lauren, who was four or five, were strolling on the pedestrian mall one day when a leather-jacketed man with multiple ear-studs approached them and asked Lauren in his snickery voice what she was up to today. There was something about Paul—and I hope he would be pleased to hear me say it—that suggested both Ron Howard (as Opie on "The Andy Griffith Show") and Truman Capote. My mother was alarmed by the leather, the hardware, and what she saw as the leer on his face.

"Don't worry, Grandma," Lauren reassured her. "Paul is one of my adult friends." He was still Paul at that time.

My children grew up with—or should I say, at—the Hamburg Inn. They were seven, four, and one-and-a-half when we came to Iowa City so that I could attend the Writer's Workshop. The combined financial blow of graduate school, moving to another state, and quitting our jobs (!) in Milwaukee left us with little—actually, with no—money for fun or child care. John found a job that allowed him to come home a little early on Tuesday afternoons so I could go to workshop, and I stayed home with the kids the rest of the week. Weather permitting, we often roamed the streets, the kids and I, Lauren in the stroller and Elizabeth toddling along—Jeff, too, if school was out. Many were the times we wound up at the Burg, sharing a booth and an order of pancakes. Jeff won a potato clock during a promotion that involved weekly drawings for prizes. The more often you came in, the better your chances. It worked, too. The clock, I mean. The electricity came from two potatoes.

When Elizabeth was six and so afraid that she would swallow the baby tooth hanging by a thread in the front of her mouth that she refused to eat, I took her to the Burg to entice her with a bowl of brown-sugared oatmeal. This was one of her favorite foods and, our waiter noted, one that she didn't need to chew. I will never forget the grateful way she looked up at us after her first mouthful, smiling bravely through her tears. The tooth was gone.

Years later, when Liz was in high school, she arranged to surprise her boyfriend with dinner at the Burg on Valentine's Day. I have a picture of them at the Presidential table, elegantly set with white tablecloth, candle, and a vase of fresh flowers, their waiter standing by in a secondhand tuxedo jacket and bow-tie, a white towel folded over his arm.

Liz was not the only Stefaniak to host a special occasion at the Hamburg Inn. When my first book came out, Prairie Lights owner Jim Harris came up with a great marketing idea. We'd have a drawing on the night I read at the bookstore, the prize a free breakfast with Jim Harris and the author at—you guessed it—Hamburg Inn No. 2. You might have had to buy a copy of *Self Storage and Other Stories* to enter, unless that was illegal in the state of Iowa, in which case, of course, no purchase was necessary.

But my literary relationship with the Burg goes back farther than that. My very first author event in Iowa City—an after-hours reading with two poets—took place at the Hamburg Inn on a Thursday at 11:30 p.m., according to the flyer still hanging on the bulletin board in my husband's office. The poets were Nancy Loeb of Tuscaloosa (she who helped me spill ice water on Millie the waitress in the ICU) and John Marshall of Seattle. While one of us used the seat of a centrally located booth for a stage, the other two served free coffee and apple pie at cost. Our publicist, fiction writer and fellow workshopper Brent Spencer, designed the flyer in the manner of a menu, featuring dishes with punning names that honored writing and writers, especially those connected with the Workshop. Faculty and visitors at the time included James Alan McPherson, Jorie Graham, Raymond Carver, Marvin Bell, Gerald Stern, Stanley Plumly, Bill Knott, and James Galvin. Jack Leggett was director of the Workshop then and David Hamilton editor of *The Iowa Review*. Breakfast offerings on our special menu included Egg McPherson, Green Eggs and Hamilton, and Graham Crackers Enjamb. For dinner, there was Carvered Turkey, Leggett of Lamb, Stuffed Bell Pepper, and Variable Pig's Feet. Apple Sternover, Plumly Pudding, and the Butterknott Sundae rounded out the dessert menu. The house wine? Le Gal Vin.

My mother came to know Iowa City quite well over the years, but during her most recent visit—the first since she'd had a stroke that compromised her short-term memory—she had to be reminded frequently of where she was, namely, Iowa City, and why (because we live there). When we asked her if she wanted to eat at the Burg, we expected the little frown, the puzzled pause. Instead, after barely a moment's thought, she said, "Home fries for me." Her usual.

Mary Helen Stefaniak's novel, *The Cailiffs of Baghdad, Georgia* (W. W. Norton), received the 2011 Anisfield-Wolf Book Award for works that make an important contribution to our understanding of racism and appreciation for the diversity of human cultures. *The Cailiffs of Baghdad, Georgia* was also an Indie-Next "Great Reads" pick for 2010. Her previous novel, *The Turk and My Mother,* received the 2005 John Gardner Fiction Award and has been translated into several languages. *Self Storage and Other Stories* (New Rivers Press) received the Wisconsin Library Association's 1998 Banta Award. An Iowa Public Radio commentator and former contributing editor for *The Iowa Review,* she divides her time between Iowa City, where she and her husband John live in a 150-year-old stagecoach inn they recently restored, and Omaha, where she teaches at Creighton University. Visit her website at www.maryhelenstefaniak.com.

☆☆☆☆☆ READING! ☆☆☆☆☆

NANCY LOEB
☞ Catch O' the Day

MARY STEFANIAK
☞ Daily Special

JOHN MARSHALL
☞ The Big Cheese All the Way

☞ Breakfast

    Eggs Benedict $2.25
    Egg McPherson $1.75
    Green Eggs and Hamilton $3.50
    Mush (Fried, Poached, Filleted) . . $ .45
    Graham Crackers Enjamb. . . . . . . $ .65

☞ Beverages

    Coffee . . . . $ .35
    More Coffee . . . . ditto
    Much More Coffee. . . . . ditto
    House Wine: Le Gal Vin. $1.00

☞ Dinner

    Carvered Turkey $2.95
    Leggett of Lamb $3.75
    Variable Pig's Feet $4.25
    Blaised Tips O' Beef. $3.60
    Chicken Special (w/ oleo & bun) . . $2.80
    Stuffed Bell Pepper $2.25
    Vegetarian Platter (Roast Beef à Dew) 2.70

☞ Dessert

    Apple Sternover. $1.25
    Dutch Apple Pie à la mode . . . . . $ .90
    Plumly Pudding . . . . $ .70
    Butterknott Sundae . . . . $ .95

AT "THE BURG"

THURSDAY 11:30 PM

FREE COFFEE AND TEA

APPLE PIE A LA MODE AT COST

☞ Due to Limited Seating Please Be Considerate Of Those Writing

Video cameraman taping a program for the History Channel

Biswamit Dwibedy

Diner

Sleep state

Alarm

uncharted and windy
enjoyment without margin
understood through disappointment
                        impressed to the morning air

                        my stanzaic water
                        turns on all sorts of
ulterior motives

                        exchanged for a lapse
                        in proximity

                        cold head buried in cooking

                        provisional limbs
                        trim the wick
                        the sweat
                         crushed, corroding
  intimacy

                        under the table
                        accidental touches
                   recreating a scenario

A.M.

    walking in

                                     —is
                              the moon today

       a delay between
arrivals, order

                               & will not look
                               you in the eye
                            will not touch
                              the skin
                                a con—

"fine" meant

                             in which
                             you can't tell
                            a fin

from the net

                            can't tell

        what they want

                            from their order

Eggs

Today's hunger used me like
instrumental syrup
a dozen eggs

strapped to waist
the food was on difficultly

difficulty
cultivated around us
          breaks   this

smoke that invites
inconsistent shade

flotsam from a myth

a movie- thinking

winter would melt
under

"heat of moment"

Heat

Back in the heat of the kitchen
Arousals unusually explained
a rush: when people come in
how he crudely "forms a fin;
a whole school" in the flipped
mirror of your eyes

moss made to look like a river
in wanderlust

 Can shimmer like
 a sheen caught in the wind
craving a landscape

Splayed under the sun

says something to himself:
Something else to the stove

I imagine you touching

mirror in which
its depths, doubles

Arthur

Our net of closeness and distance
"in a ball of yarn" or fabric of
fold by fold that unravels Arthur
 singing—your understanding

It was a way of saying I want you
also to have the same experience.

A lens through which we look at
touch where his lips had listed
possibilities waiting at the door

 you wouldn't have recognized
or even know that I was there

Rustle

                                                            always at hand yet impossible to touch
                                                           phrases that match the moment perfectly

                                                    continuity of the melodic line as a back
    ground emotion with twice the air

  indulgent as a husband but not
                                              faithful distance voice didn't fade into

                                    a response to particulars was a rock carved
                                            desire's accumulating delays
                                    between weather & refusal to speak
                                    when he rudely shouts out what he wants
                                              & my life is not a personal thing-

I think of us as friends
                                                      but not so early in the morning

Dear Sam

Attraction rubs off.
 You are
constantly touching the man I love.

Touches characteristic of a manuscript
 but not touches that indicate an author.

In an ancient book I read, the body is considered
a meeting place of all the touches

I depend on accidents while often touching
my own lips. These accidents I use
as a rule of thumb: whence and how they came

to be pleased and to please. My flesh beating
times suddenly still; confusions
body can't remember; knowing that is simply
transitions on the screen

I said I but what I mean is my daughter, writer
sits and floats—"love is the grand use
one person rips of another"—

 between songs
 and dull parts of the afternoon

would be seen coming out of his house.

Body

(for Rosmarie Waldrop)

The voice opens to the body
but the body cannot keep the voice

I thought it were otherwise

my hopes were crushed by this knowledge

Outside, a crowd unbuttoned into exclamations
                                        exposed himself
  glittering
on a spider-web

"all this is in the present
& in the mirror, every night

possibilities predicting
a tongue caught in
grain of sentences

I had badly wanted a story of my own

Not a body but a one
without boundary or edge

Voice

    contained in the trivial
    something ancient, with no intention

     a voice can cling to you
      in the middle of a sentence
   & pacing back and forth
           your window, weather
 acknowledged as an accomplice.

eyes seen differently creating a path now
       for the moon just beginning to come up in
        in these books I have called my home
     & morning somewhere else

      I hear his voice takes
  where a wing would form

In another myth
 he'd have swallowed the sun.

His horoscope said it would taste like
   any other fruit, when I thought
it was more like an egg
    he was about to crack.

Rush

Our acts are mistakes
but nobody tells you
regulars regulate joy
 in what one does
thrive in the lack of

touching repeatedly
calls out my name
or curse I mishear

 the noise drenched
already in someone
else's attention.

                                                                                    A stir
                                                                           under the rush
fingers' spiral   an eye on each

                                         hands on fire—
                                         crowds collecting
                                                                           clouds the color of

sweat—
                                screaming
                            I love my job!

                                                                                                            Fur

Your eggs are lovely Hubble

Unfurling at what speed
 are moving away from one another

he knows good food arouses & inspires
& anything sung is always in the present tense.

Driving by we saw signs of ruined nations
and dreams in which you resembled an animal

& had found extreme comfort in the plush hide

Carnage of my collaborative seductions

noon again
o blinding
 lane/law/n
   America is unreal
a bodied thump
      rides on
                            turning the air green.

 And gather, hidden, on a window: a grassy gown:
this notion of a home you would have laughed at.

Swollen red river, moves along the corner of
strike and it's an electric, incapable geometry

An airy place unique to each artery
—this is that.   This was that
which emits at night.   Clear as Vodka &
oiling down the wind with your two names.

To the coming together of their meaning in a sentence
are a river falling over. Incomprehensible men
Will crush it up in a rage

and tied to his wrist
bones floating in the sound

      I said the road destroys me
but going away I will take an inventory

Skin

what wills unfold
gilded on a glacier

in utterances common and untrue
the news is a déjà vu

Glass that orchestrates a long division

I saw him get into a blue van

I think the eyes are a museum

of salt drying on lashes where
I serve underneath
sail in & wets his beak in my
stream of
lover of
fragments

"single men and their single meals"

Cheering the team into an embrace
abridged into a single week's victory

        a wick's
    reversal of my desire for
another skin going on

it's a mistake that holds the bridges together.

And if you remember it extends
through watery flowers of a unique self
cutting into borders

A scene in which our city is flooded

& I leave you with your two friends

                    Just us girls

              Pretending to be on t.v.
              Dialogue/resemblance
              Brunch order structures
              Replicated where are my
              Home fries the guest a
                              good tipper
              the oil burns deeper
              on your fingertips

Biswamit Dwibedy is from Orissa, India, and currently lives in Bangalore. He has a MFA from Bard College, New York. He also lived in Iowa City for several years. These poems were written during his time working at the Hamburg Inn when he used fragments of overheard customers' conversations, along with other material, collaged together to create a fictional-autobiography in verse. The Diner Series is excerpted from Dwibedy's second book *Hubble Gardner* (forthcoming); some of the poems have appeared in *The Recluse* and *1913*, 3 & 4.

The Romance of the Table and Chair

Poet/artist Dave Morice has been coming to Hamburg Inn No. 2 since the 1970s and has often sketched there; his impromptu sketches are scattered throughout the book—this set is from 1978.

Robert Garner McBrearty

The Dishwasher

I'm a dishwasher in a restaurant. I'm not trying to impress anybody. I'm not bragging. It's just what I do. It's not the glamorous job people make it out to be. Sure, you make a lot of dough and everybody looks up to you and respects you, but then again there's a lot of responsibility. It weighs on you. It wears on you. Everybody wants to be a dishwasher these days, I guess, but they've got an idealistic view of it.
"Come on, kid, come on, kid, hustle, hustle, move 'em," the manager's calling in that friendly, staccato voice of his, pushing me on. "Move 'em, kid, rinse that crap off, first into the side sink, we don't want all that grease and stuff in the main sink, c'mon, hustle! We're getting behind!"
The waiters, waitresses, cook, are there now, too, right behind him, cheering me on.
"C'mon, we need some silverware, we need some plates, we got people waiting, they're getting fierce out there. Give me a goddamn plate for Christ's sake."
"Okay, kid," the manager says. "After you rinse off all that ketchup and chicken bones into the side sink, throw the plates and stuff into the soapy water in the main sink. Let 'em soak. Now as they're soaking, dig in there, that's right, dig in there and-"
"Into all that grime and gray-black sudsy water, sir?" I ask.
"That's right. Scoop for the ones that have been soaking. Scoop!" He makes a scooping motion with his hand.
"I think this one's ready, sir."
"What's that? Egg yolk…I see egg yolk on that, Christ, get that off."
The cook shouts in that cheerful, chiding voice of his, "You turkey! I got eggs ready, I got hamburgers, I got fries, I got onion rings, I got grease popping up into my eyes, but I don't have a lousy plate to put anything on. Turkey!" The cook respects me a lot, and knows I take it in stride. He mumbles and swears some more, but I know that's just his style when he's tense.
"All right, kid." The manager's bent over with me now. We're both bent right over that steaming, bubbling, smelly sink together. He's got his top button loose. I can see the sweat pouring off of his face. He's breathing heavy, but his face is dead set and calm now, though I know what's going on under the surface. I respect him for his self-control since he has a generally florid personality.
"Okay, kid, how ya feeling?"
"I'm okay," I say.
"You got your mind on something today, don't you?"
I shake my head. "I'm just getting warm."

A server during the lunch shift

"You don't seem like you're really with it."

A plate squirts out of my soapy, slippery hands. I grab for it, knock it back up in the air, it twirls, the manager grabs for it, and sends it twisting back up in the other direction, I grab for it again, but it slides through my hands like I'm trying to grab a fish in the water, and lands with a sick-sounding clang and breaks into pieces on the floor.

The manager looks at me and coughs. He sort of stares up at the ceiling for awhile, as if wondering if it's ready for a new paint job. I watch the colors in his face change to red. I know he feels as badly about this as I do.

"Thank God it wasn't a glass," I say, "those really bust into bits."

"Are you happy here?" he asks me.

"Sure."

"I mean, are you really happy?"

The manager takes a personal as well as a professional interest in me. I respect him for that. "Of course," I say, "who wouldn't be?"

"Okay, we're going to forget about that one," he says. "It was just a plate." He gives a funny sort of laugh, short violent bursts of air, as if someone is standing behind him and giving him bear hugs.

"I don't mean to be rude," Sally, the waitress, comes back to say, "but people are really getting downright hostile. Some fellow out there is claiming he's having a low blood sugar attack. Can't we at least get them some coffee?"

The manager breathes. "Okay, let's start from scratch again. A whole new ballgame. You give the cups just a quick rinse. Okay, just a quick rinse, and then you put them on that tray, and then you run them through the machine, one cycle, takes a minute, you take them out of the machine, you carry the tray out to the front where the waitress can get to them. Okay?"

"What tray?"

"That one."

"Oh. The blue one?"

He makes a funny little sound again, sort of a cross between laughing and gagging. "Yeah," he says, taking me suddenly by the arm in an affectionate gesture and leading me to the tray in question. He takes my hand in his in a fatherly way and places it on the tray. He rubs my hand across the tray so that I will get a good feel of it.

"Hard rubber?" I say.

"That's right. Hard rubber," he says.

"It doesn't melt in the machine?"

"No. Never. This is the tray that you will use. This is the tray that you will run through the machine with the coffee cups on it."

"Oh, okay," I say.

We bend back over the sink. The steam rises into my nostrils and I give a little laugh.

"What's funny?" the manager asks.

"I think of Macbeth. You know, the witch's cauldron."

"Oh, you think of Macbeth."

"I saw the movie," the cook calls. "Pretty weird." He gives a high pitched laugh. I know he's stoned.
Sally comes back. "I'm not going back out there," she says. "I'm the one who has to take all the guff when something isn't ready. I'm not going back out there until I can give them something."
"Tell them some jokes," the cook calls. "Do a little dance for them, Sally baby."
"I just wish somebody would tell me what's going on back here."
"Look, we got some paper cups," the manager says. "Stall them, give them some water in paper cups."
"Water in paper cups, beautiful," she says.
"One time in Atlanta," the cook starts.
"Oh, shut up," the manager says. "Just cook and shut up."
The cook slams down his spatula. "You riding me, man? You want me to walk off? You want me to walk off right now?"
"Lay off, Charlie. I didn't mean anything."
"You riding me?"
"Forget it. Okay? I'm sorry."
"You can do the cooking, you like it so much," he mumbles. But he goes back to flipping the hamburger patties. The manager and the cook always have a friendly, lively, give-and-take. I respect their relationship a lot.
"Okay kid, how we doing?" the manager says, rolling up his shirt sleeves. He edges in next to me at the sink, and stares at me, intent, and asks, looking down now at the gray stinking water, "You want me to go in there with you? You want me to go down in there with you?"
I put a tentative hand into the water. I go down a few inches. Something heavy, with a harsh, leathery feel butts up against my hand, and I jerk back. You never know what's floating around down there. I take a deep breath though, and say, "I'll handle it. I'll do it. Let me just try it my way."
He sighs heavily. He looks suddenly tired and old. "Okay, give it a go."
And I do. The plates come back with ketchup smeared across them, chicken bones, crumpled napkins, bits of bread dripping gravy, cigarettes snuffed out in egg yolks, mutilated French fries. I knock the paper and bones and ashes off into the trash can under the sink. Then I give a quick rinse in the side sink to get the main crap off, then I drop the plates into the sudsy water of the main sink to soak off any crusty stuff. I scoop back into the sink, pull something out, give a quick wipe, and then put everything on a tray and run it through the machine. Meanwhile, waiting for the machine to finish its cycle, I keep up with the other stuff, knock the crap off, rinse, soak, scoop, wipe. The machine gives a buzz. I throw it open. Great clouds of steam boil my facial flesh. Sort the plates, silverware, glasses, cups. Run the plates over to the cook. Run the glasses and cups out front where the waitress can get to them. The waitress runs back, grabs the plates from the cook that he's just filled with food, meanwhile crying out, "Two fries, three deluxe burgers, one without onions, two chicken dinners, substitute peas for corn on one of them."
"Substitute peas for corn," the cook repeats scornfully. He doesn't respect people who want substitutions.
But I'm really moving now. Trash off. Crap off. Rinse. Soak. Scoop. Wipe. Machine. Remove. Sort. Run over to the cook. I'm moving

and the manager's calling out in his staccato voice, "Okay, kid, now we're going, now we're going, keep 'em moving, way to go kid, keep it up, we're catching up now," and out of the corner of my eye I catch the cook giving me a quick glance and nodding his head approvingly. The kid's okay, he's thinking, the kid's going to be okay. Sally, hustling by, gives me a little pat on the shoulder. "Okay," she says, "Okay." I respect her and may be falling in love with her.
The manager's grinning now. "Okay, doing a good job tonight, boys, yes sir. We're starting to do a good job. How we coming on the chicken, Charlie?"
"Chicken's okay," he says, "let's move the potatoes."
"I could move the potatoes," I say, "where do you want them?"
"No, kid, that's okay." The manager calls to Sally, "Move the potatoes. How's the cole slaw?"
"They ain't going for the cole slaw," Charlie says. "Day cook put too much mayonnaise. You got to watch the mayonnaise on the cole slaw."
We're going, yes sir, I'm hot. I'm really hot. I'm sweating and shaking, but I'm moving fast, and the manager even says, "Hey, slow it down, don't kill yourself."
"No sir, I won't, I'm okay."
You can feel it when a restaurant's moving. Everybody's working in synchronization. You hear dishes and forks rattling, grease hissing. You feel like you're beating them. And them's the customers. The customers are out to get you and you're out to get them, and if you make them happy, you've beaten them.
"Slow it down, kid, slow it down," the manager says. "Don't burn yourself out."
And then Sally comes back into the grill area, and we all know, before she's said anything, that something's gone wrong.
"What is it, Sally?" the manager asks.
Slowly, she raises up a silver spoon for all of us to see. "Greasy," she says. "Somebody sent it back. Said it was greasy."
She looks down. None of us say anything. The cook whistles and turns back to his burgers, flipping them slowly and methodically. The manager takes the spoon from her, and tosses it back into the gray-black sudsy water. "Wash it again for the clown out there," he says.
I go back to my dishes, but I feel sick and disappointed inside. Later though the manager takes me aside and says gruffly, "It wasn't your fault. Don't get down. It was a tough break. The wrong spoon, the wrong guy…"
Later, down in the basement, I talk to the famous old janitor, who is mopping with slow, steady strokes.
"You like it here?" I ask. "You like the work?"
"Ah, I used to," he says. "I liked the reputation, you know. I liked the girls that came with it."
"But you don't like it anymore?"
"Ah, now it's just money. Everybody's just in it for the money. And I go along with them. I take what I can get. But I always loved it too. I was pretty good in my day." He sweeps his hand around at the clean looking rows of canned goods. "It all starts down here with me, you know. I make a mistake one day and it's all up. Yeah, I'm tired of the responsibility. I think I'm going to hang it up pretty soon."

"What will you do then?"

"I'm thinking of getting me a condominium in Vail. I've got a hell of a lot put away over the years." He chuckles and runs a hand through his thin white hair. "I guess I did all right after all."

I watch him go on mopping, mopping with even, steady, sliding strokes that show me that while he has never been truly gifted, not gifted in the way I sense I am in my field, he has made up for it with dedication, reliability, and respect.

"The Dishwasher" was Robert Garner McBrearty's first published story, written while he was a student at the Iowa Writers' Workshop. The story went on to win a Pushcart Prize. Robert says, "After a night of washing dishes at the Hamburg Inn, I wrote the first draft in longhand from about midnight to five in the morning, collapsed, and when I woke up later, I could barely read my writing. But what I could read seemed not too bad. I loved my time at the Burg, the people, the sights, the sounds. It was a good contrast to school. And I learned the great art of dishwashing." Robert's fiction has been widely published in such places as the *Pushcart Prize, Missouri Review, North American Review, Narrative, New England Review,* and many other literary journals. He is the author of two collections of short stories, *A Night at the Y*; and *Episode*, which won the Sherwood Anderson Foundation Fiction Award. A new book, *Let the Birds Drink in Peace*, is being published by Conundrum Press. He teaches writing at the University of Colorado.

When current general manager Steve Fugate began working at the Hamburg Inn No. 2 at the age of 15 [1980], his co-workers were all "old ladies in smocks" who would occasionally chase him around with brooms. "If I didn't have the place shining by 3 p.m., I was in trouble," Fugate said, chuckling. Approximately 10 years after his first day on the job, he was promoted to general manager. Fugate met his wife of seven years, Wende, at the restaurant in the mid-1990s. "Wende was such a good cook he couldn't let her get away," he said. Binegar, *The Daily Iowan,* November 15, 2005

Joe and his tattoo of *The Thinker,* after hours

The waitstaff has always served as a gauge of the times. In the early 70s, you most likely would have been served by a hard left politico in overalls. In the early 80s, waiters sporting technicolor mohawks were the norm. Last time I was there, an Iowa-bred blonde bearing Rastilocks brought me my burger. Pretty much anything goes. Mohr, *icon,* June 1995

An appreciated tip

Larry Baker

Am I an old-timer yet?

Am I an old-timer in Iowa City yet? I've been here 30 years. But I've only known the Hamburg Inn since it moved to its current Linn Street location. I can remember my first meal there. I know it was my first because I was specifically told to go there for the hamburger and fries. My source did not mention the ambience. Nor did he give me any history. "You want a good burger, you gotta go there." That's all. And I kept going back.

Over time, I settled into a basic menu. The burger was a constant, and then I started eating breakfast there too. Always an omelet. Thursdays were a special day: the fried chicken dinner. Hamburgers, eggs, and fried chicken…you did not go to the Burg for exotic food. And you could usually expect to stand and wait if you went at dinner time.

Was it the best food in Iowa City? Not really, George's has better burgers, the old Pearson's Drugstore counter had better milk shakes, but the Burg was not a food destination as much as it was a social destination. It was an odd melting pot of "types" in a college town. Artists and anti-establishment long-hairs and tattooed diners, and that was before piercing became a fad. University staff and faculty too. Eating there was like buying a Volvo, part of the image. But also the world of Norman Rockwell and Ronald Reagan. Blond and pony-tailed sorority girls, but never dressed for a date. No, these were social club young men and women up too early in the morning after a night of partying. Casual clothes thrown on by those puffy-eyed kids who just wanted breakfast and enough caffeine to jolt them into a new day. Being served by a Goth waitress who was probably twice as smart.

Most college towns have their own version of Hamburg Inn. Some example of an older more individual America. No uniforms on the staff there. You could see and hear the kitchen. Blue plate specials. After awhile, especially with those who come to the college town for school but stay for other reasons, a place like the Hamburg Inn becomes an inorganic form of comfort food. Part of your past, idealized and returned to, and, as you sit down in a booth or at the counter, you inhale the aroma of your own memory.

Larry Baker has lived in Iowa City since 1980. In that time, he served two terms on the City Council, published three novels, and earned his PhD in English from the University of Iowa. His fourth novel will be published in 2012.

Luke placing an order in the computer

Laurel Snyder

Technology

Trying to grow a machine from inside this flower—

is like trying to grow a flower from inside this machine.
I don't believe in silver petals, in leaves unfolding like tender cogs.
I don't believe in hybrids, in the shiny cyborg bouquet.

I'm obsessed with this.

My dream therapist would say, "I'm totally fascinated
by your erratic behavior and your uncanny self-awareness.
I can't possibly fix you, but by all means, continue."

My name is Laurel and I'll be your waitress this evening—

When I get to the table with the big ugly menus, a fat woman is drinking
straight from the scratched water pitcher on the table, so I set down a glass
in front of her and I say, "Ma'am, why are you drinking from that water pitcher?

because we all have to drink from that, you know—"

Now it's time to go to bed. I'm wearing just my bra, so it's almost me.
You're reading a blue paperback, and when I stretch out beside you, peer down,
run my hand over my own breasts, cup my own belly, I say,

"Look at this senseless landscape from where I am. See?"

Reprinted from *Born Magazine*, 2005.

I'm a restaurant.

I'm a restaurant but not an establishment. I'm a window. A tired one. With an arm reaching through to ask, "Where are those fries? I asked for them twenty minutes ago. What's the goddamn holdup?"

It was raining and now it isn't anymore but the floor is a puddle and tiled and so—still—disaster!

This window is not a window
To the outside. Some aren't.
Sometimes there's no view.

Laurel Snyder is the author of many books for grownups and children, including a picture book called *Inside the Slidy Diner* and a children's novel, *Any Which Wall*. Both were both inspired at least in part by her time at the Hamburg Inn No. 2. Laurel lives with her family in Atlanta, GA and online at http://laurelsnyder.com

"The counter, the vibe, the crunchiness—I pictured the Hamburg when I wrote it [*Slidy Diner,* her children's book about a diner], I worked at the Hamburg during my time at the [Writers'] Workshop, and, frankly, that place kept me sane. I think the macabre nature of *Slidy Diner* represents my emotional state at the time. I was lost and trying to figure things out." Howe, *Little Village,* November 2008, quoting former waitress Laurel Synder

"Nobody's out of place here," said David [Panther], as customers ambled in early today. 'There's everybody, from people with no money to millionaires." Heth, *Iowa City Press-Citizen,* October 1983

The 1990 update

Fire !

Fire broke out before dawn on April 17, 1994 and burned for five and a half hours.

Part of exposed ceiling and wall, perhaps going back to the era when the building was a meat market.

"The fire was called in at about 4:35 a.m..." [Dave] Cohen [co-manager] says. "To the best of their ability, the fire department has determined that it started in our recycling area outside the building, specifically in a box of cardboard. Thankfully, the majority of the damage in the restaurant was limited to the back wall of the kitchen. In all, the rough estimate of damage caused by the fire is over $100,000." Cohen says that it was a difficult fire to extinguish. "The building is 100 years old with heavy construction between two brick walls," he adds. "First of all, the storage area was totally destroyed in back, so we'll be building a 25-by 20-foot addition to the building. That will become our new prep kitchen," Cohen explains. [Co-manager Steve] Fulgate says that the Hamburg Inn also will be adding some seating, bringing its total capacity to 63 diners." Risch, *The Hawk's Eye*, Summer 1994

A glimpse into what had been the cooler

"We're not really sure—we think some drunk might've flipped a cigarette butt into our recycling bin," Fugate said. [Coralville, West Branch and Solon firefighters assisted.] Sunderbruch, *The Daily Iowan,* April 1994

After an early morning fire on April 17 ...the restaurant reopened on June 5, complete with expanded kitchen and seating areas. A grand reopening celebration is planned for this weekend, June 18 and 19. Sunderbruch, *The Daily Iowan,* April 1994

Fire fails to close down Hamburg Inn tradition

By Heather Sloman Woodin

IOWA CITY — One of Dave Panther's biggest frustrations in the aftermath of an April 17 restaurant fire was not knowing who started the blaze.

The fire, which has been ruled suspicious, closed the Hamburg Inn No. 2 for almost seven weeks.

The fire caused about $150,000 in damage.

PANTHER'S FAMILY opened the restaurant 46 years ago, and Panther never considered not reopening the eatery after the fire.

Panther also is co-owner of the Funny Business theatrical shop and is a part-time professional clown. That's his true love.

The fire could have brought an end to the Hamburg Inn, allowing Panther to turn all his attention to the store and clowning, but he stuck with it and rebuilt.

"It would be very difficult to just say 'I'm through. There will be no more Hamburg Inn.' It would be especially hard on my father, who ran the restaurant for years before Dave Panther took over.

"When he heard about the fire, the first thing that he had heard was that it had already burned down. He was much relieved to talk to me and learn it was bad but not a disaster," Panther said.

Hamburg Inn is the "financial anchor" that allows Panther to pursue other interests, he said. "Food service is not the thing that gives me the charge out of life that the clown end of it does, but it certainly provides the opportunity to explore these areas and still have the financial support.

"For years and years, I worked for the restaurant instead of making the restaurant work for me," Panther said.

The restaurant at 214 N. Linn St. reopened June 4 with a bigger kitchen and food preparation area.

> *"It would be very difficult to just say 'I'm through. There will be no more Hamburg Inn.' It would be especially hard on my father, who ran the restaurant for years before Dave Panther took over."*
>
> **Dave Panther, Hamburg Inn owner**

Above: Heather Sloman Woodin reported on the fire in the *Cedar Rapids Gazette,* August 1994. Right: Another fire was reported in the *Iowa City Press-Citizen* on December 21, 1948, at Hamburg Inn #1 while Mrs. Sophia Amrine was making chili in a pressure cooker.

IOWA CITY P

IN THIS SECTION — Local News, Sports, Want Ads, Comics

TUESDAY, DECEMBER 21, 1948

EMPLOYE HURT IN EXPLOSION

Pressure Blows Off Lid of Cooker in Local Eating House

Mrs. Sophie Amrine, 427 South Van Buren street, was injured shortly after 7 p.m. Monday at Hamburg Inn No. 1, 119 Iowa avenue, when a large pressure cooker full of chili soup blew up in her face.

The explosion splattered hot liquid on Mrs. Amrine's face, threw her to the floor and shattered windows and door glass of the eating house.

Mrs. Amrine was given first-aid treatment by a physician and is recovering satisfactorily today at her home. Her injuries are not critical.

Firemen were called to the scene, but the explosion did not result in a blaze. They said apparently a valve on the cooker became stopped up, allowing pressure to build up until it blew off the lid.

Mrs. Amrine, an employe of the inn, came to work at 7 p.m. and said she "hadn't been there two minutes when the thing blew up." She was about two feet from the cooker.

The establishment is owned by Adrian Panther.

Pressure Cooker Explodes, One Injured

WHEN A PRESSURE COOKER (indicated by arrow) blew up Monday evening at Hamburg Inn No. 1, 119 Iowa Avenue, it injured a woman employe, smashed out several windows including the big front glass shown here and scattered hot chili soup through the interior of the establishment. (Press-Citizen Photo).

Exterior, 1950s

Mary Ryan Hogen, with her husband Tom, stopped in while on a visit to Iowa City. She graduated from Mercy's nursing program 50 years ago. She says she frequented the Hamburg Inn and that "it was the best place in town." Tom attended the University of Iowa and later sold Lance food products to the Burg. Personal communication

Tom and Mary Ryan Hogen

Gary Sanders

'A restaurant with a soul'

In April 1979, a short, scruffy-looking guy came in to Hamburg Inn looking for a job. He was not particularly optimistic about his chances.
He'd been unemployed since he arrived in Iowa City the previous November, and earlier that morning he'd walked out of Maid-Rite after glancing at their six-page application. Six pages for a waiter's job? Even in the most educated city in the United States, that was a bit much.

Maybe it was time to forget about Iowa City and go back to Michigan. But first he'd try The Burg. If they didn't hire him, at least he could get a decent cup of coffee and read a stray newspaper.
When he asked the waitress about a job, she said "Dave's in back," and ushered him into a very cluttered little room surrounded by shelves filed with huge cans of ketchup and large cardboard boxes labeled "paper cups," and "napkins." The smell of grilled hamburgers permeated every nook and cranny.

A man of about 30 with thinning sandy-colored hair sat at a small cleared-off area. He appeared to be going over the books. "You ever been a waiter before?" he asked.
"Yeah, back in Detroit, a few years ago."
Dave peered at the job-seeker for maybe 10 seconds.
"All right. Come in tonight at 6 p.m., and we'll try you out."

That was it. No interview, no six-page application. No application at all. Just the basic question—can you do the job.
When I left Hamburg Inn that morning I wondered if I could survive my dinner hour trial.
Two years later I served my last burger and fries. And, except for the chicken grease clogging my sinuses on Sundays, and one very demanding obnoxious customer, it was a great experience.

When I started working there I had no friends in Iowa City. Two years later I knew waitresses, cooks, teachers, doctors, carpenters, salesmen, postal workers, and artists. I was part of the community.
And Dave was the kind of boss everyone hopes to work for. He never raised his voice, and he never asked any personal questions like

"Late night at the Hamburg Inn, Gary Sanders" circa 1979

"why is a guy who used to be a school teacher working in a joint like this?" If you did your job, that was enough.

If you occasionally messed up an order, well, anyone could make a mistake once in a while. I you wanted to go to school for a semester, he'd work out the schedule. If you left town for a month or two, he'd take you back. And if you needed a little cash until payday, he'd help you out. It's been eight years since I worked at the Burg. Not much has changed there. A few more people around the country know about it because it's been praised in a book by Susan Stamberg of National Public Radio and in the bible of two-lane highways, *Road Food*.

But now the old Burg is closed for remodeling. The very idea of a renovated Hamburg Inn makes many people nervous. Will the oldest family-owned restaurant in Iowa City resemble McDonald's when they re-open Monday?
Let's hope not. Hamburg Inn has something sadly lacking in today's restaurants: a soul. It truly is one of Iowa City's treasures.
And for me, it's more than that. If Dave Panther hadn't hired that short, scruffy-looking guy 11 years ago, Iowa City would not have become my home. One of a series of biweekly columns for the *Iowa City Press-Citizen*, dated February 14, 1990

Gary Sanders is a teacher, writer and activist.

"Hamburg Inn Only Located in Iowa City!!!

Cedar Rapids,	No	London,	Not Here
Des Moines,	No Way	Davenport,	Wrong
Chicago,	Not	Kansas City,	Wrong Again
St. Louis,	Dah	Paris,	Not There

Other Not Cities Available on Request
Check National Geographical Survey!!!"

Hamburg Inn #2-Memories of a Special Place

I moved to Iowa City from Ann Arbor in 1978 and I was sort of floating through life, trying to figure out which way to go, when I was hired as a waiter at Hamburg Inn #2 in April, 1979, and I worked there until 1981. The folks who had opened the diner in 1948, Fritz and Fran Panther, still worked there occasionally. Their son Dave, who was the manager, worked a lot of hours, including whatever grunt work was necessary—which I really respected him for. Dave's aunt, Pauline Hamm, was a waitress, as was Pat Hinkle, who had started working there after graduating from high school in 1957 (and stayed until retirement in 1997). They were dedicated, friendly professional waitresses, and they were very patient with the "new kid." I also worked with the legendary waitress Mickey, short and rotund, whose booming voice I can still hear as she approached me carrying plates of food while I was waiting on a customer in the cramped space behind the counter: "Behind ya', coming in."

I was 32 years old when I started working there, and I was younger than all of these folks (though just a few months younger than Dave). That's the big difference between The Burg then and now—the waitstaff is much younger, and the customers are younger. It was more of a blue collar place back then, and, of course, there's been a lot of modernization. Back then we only had booths and counter, no tables. And, believe it or not, customers were not only allowed to smoke, but we sold cigarettes!

Along with the waitstaff there were the cooks and dishwashers, some of whom are still around Iowa City—Robert Deblois, Scotty Hayward, Jeffrey Morgan (and even though Robert McBrearty teaches in Colorado, he lives on at The Burg through his short story "The Dishwasher"). We were open until 1:00 am on Friday and Saturday nights, and sometimes in the summer when it took us a couple of hours to clean up the place, we'd sit outside and drink a few beers and wait for the sun to come up. What a time.

Considering how many different types of people I waited on, it's remarkable that there was only one customer I didn't get along with. He was a really large man, about 60. He drove a beautiful 1956 green Buick and he came in every night with his mother and sat in booth 5 in back. Back then, when customers ordered fried chicken, we had to take the pieces of raw chicken out of the back cooler, bread them and put them in the fryer for 20 minutes. This guy ordered a chicken breast and a thigh every night, and every night he wanted me to bring out the raw breast and thigh for him to inspect before I put it into the fryer. He and his mother stayed for about 2 hours and kept me hopping with numerous requests for more water. And he always left me a tip of 25 cents.

But I really had fun working there. One night one of my regular customers, a grad student of some sort, complained about the small portion of mashed potatoes I'd given him with his Roast Beef Special. So I took his plate back and scooped the largest mountain of mashed potatoes that could fit on his plate and brought it out to him. We both laughed hysterically (maybe you had to be there).

One customer changed my life. Lynn Feekin was the director of the University of Iowa Labor Center, and we had worked on a couple of labor/political projects together. One morning in August, 1980, as I served her "the usual"—fried egg, juice, toast and coffee, she said: "Hey, you were a teacher in Michigan, would you like to be a graduate assistant at the Labor Center?" And that was the job interview. Though I only worked at the Labor Center for two years, I started down the path I'm still on (with a few missteps, of course). It is mind-boggling when I contemplate my life in a parallel universe, if Lynn hadn't offered me a job that morning.

But there was also tragedy at The Hamburg. I only worked a few times with Dave's brother Mike before he was killed by a drunk driver on December 27, 1985. He was a great guy. The plaque memorializing him is on the outside wall by the parking lot. Mike's death almost destroyed Dave. But he took a year off from the Burg and went to clown school, and that helped save him. He became Babaloon the Clown, which took him into an entirely different world, away from the Hamburg. He's still occasionally performing as Babaloon, and he is still one of the few bosses that I ever had who I consider a friend.

Steve Fugate was another of the Burg's legendary people. Though I'd stopped working there in 1981, I continued to be a regular customer, and I saw him put his heart and soul into the place for 25 years. His leaving is best left for him and Dave to tell, if they choose to. Before he left (and especially afterwards) he became a local pioneer in the biodiesel movement and is now director of the environmental group I-RENEW.

One other old Burg regular I have to mention is Carl Schlueter. Though he doesn't hang out there any more, he was a regular in the early 1990's. I had a political talk show on Public Access Television, The Sanders Group, and shortly after Ronald Reagan came into the Burg in 1992, one of the staff told me that while Carl was drinking his coffee, he refused to shake Reagan's hand when the former president walked down the counter greeting everyone. I didn't know Carl, but I tracked him down and he explained: "I just didn't want to shake the SOB's hand. He was a liar and a terrible president." So that week at the end of my tv show, I announced that it was Carl Schlueter Day in Iowa City. We became friends, and I introduced him to a small-time bookie who also hung out at the Burg. Carl and I spent many Saturday afternoons watching college football, jumping up and down trying to get the teams we bet on to make us a little money. I haven't seen Carl much since the feds busted the gambling operation a few years ago, but I still admire him for not shaking Reagan's hand.

I missed Reagan's visit, but I did get to meet Bill Clinton at the Burg. It was a morning in November, 2007, about six weeks before the caucus. I sat down at the counter for a cup of coffee, and there weren't too many other customers. I looked at the table about 10 feet across from me, and there was Bill Clinton with four advisors surrounding him. There was no media or crowds of people, so I realized this wasn't a scheduled campaign stop for Hillary. I drank my coffee and tried to eavesdrop on their conversation. At one point I heard Clinton saying something about the Arkansas football team and I raised my voice just enough to be heard and said to the group: "Wasn't that triple overtime loss to Mississippi State last Saturday night a heart-breaker?" Clinton got up from his table—he was a lot taller than I'd expected—and came over to me and we talked a little college football. Absolutely no mention of politics. I asked one of the Hamburg staff to take our picture, and when he put his arm around my shoulders I felt that overwhelming personal magnetism that people have noted for years.

........It's hard to believe that it's been 32 years---half of my life and a little more than half of the Hamburg's life--since I started working there. I wrote a *Press-Citizen* column about the Burg in 1990 (reprinted in this book) mentioning how I was worried that the remodeling of the Hamburg might ruin it. But the remodeling, which has continued occasionally for 20 years, hasn't ruined it. It has a little different feel to it than when I worked there, but it's still a great place to eat and hang out. The Panther family and all the people who have worked and eaten there since 1948 have created a place that captures the spirit of Iowa City, and I just hope I'm here to celebrate the Burg's 80th anniversary in 2028.

2011

Chris' legs

This poem and others that follow are a set of impromptu poems written by guests to celebrate the restaurant's 60th Anniversary and the poetry in all of us:

The Poem

Hamburg Inn
Happiness Outt!

David Porter, 2009

Aaron Hall Holmgren, artist, working on *Ghost Bee,* a graphic novel

Shana Kaska, artist

Dick Vitosh was attending City High in 1953, the year his mother died. He'd had a series of jobs, a paper route and setting up bowling pins, but then took a job working at the Miller Mobile station on the corner of Iowa Avenue and Dodge Street, within walking distance of the Hamburg Inn. He began stopping by for a hamburger and fries and the occasional malt. Fifty-eight years later he's the patron with the longest record of eating at the diner. He said that "fresh meat made the difference" between the Burg and other restaurants. In those days, waitresses were older, polite women in their 40s and 50s—he thought mostly relatives. Not like today, when he "gets on someone's case once in awhile" for poor service.

He remembers stopping in for a burger after the Saturday night dances in Swisher, Sueyville, the Cedar Rapids dance hall and the Highland Palace in Riverside. He had completed two and a half years of college, including ROTC, when he was drafted and spent the years 1958-1962 in the air force, stationed at a base in Kunsun, Korea, where B47 bombers and other planes were being activated for Viet Nam. After maintaining radar sights and flight lights for 16 months, he returned home and he and a buddy chose to work together at the DX station on Burlington and Clinton Streets, still within distance of calling up an order to the Burg. He said Fritz was always thinking up improvements and trying to expand the space for more tables. "The menu has changed, but the service and food are the same." He said he'd be returning here until he passes on. Personal communication

Liz, manager, arranging merchandise

COME CELEBRATE 50's WEEK

OCT. 13 Thru OCT. 19

HAMBURG INN NO. 2 INC. IOWA CITY, IOWA

Iowa City's Oldest Family Owned Restaurant Since 1948

OPEN 7 DAYS A WEEK

SERVING:
• Hamburgers • Tenderloins • Chicken • Homemade Soups
• Seafood • Omlettes • Eggs • Cakes

214 N. Linn 337-5512

IOWA CITY'S FIFTIES TIME CAPSULE OF GOOD EATING!

Anniversary Celebrations Through the Years

ALL WEEK LONG

DAILY DRAWINGS FOR HAMBURG IN... AND THE AMAZING TWO POTATO CL... 32oz. CHERRY COKE IN A TAKE H... TIC CHERRY COKE CONTAINER FOR... 32oz. OF ANY FOUNTAIN DRINK I... HOME CHERRY COKE CONTAINER FO... BE LISTENING TO KRNA 93 FM RA... T-SHIRT AND GIFT COUPON GIVE... WEEK LONG.

...AY OCT. 13

...FOR T-SHIRT AND CLOCK DRAWIN... ...OKE IN 32oz. TAKE HOME ...ER ONLY 55¢. ...NTAIN DRINK IN 32oz. TAKE HOM... ...ER ONLY 55¢. ...E CREAM SANDWICHES WITH ANY ...RCHASE!

it's our 25th BIRTHDAY

Help us celebrate!

Yes, 25 years ago, two green kids came to Iowa City to start frying hamburgers for a living.

Thanks to you, our customers, we are still going strong, and we wish to invite you to share our celebration.

Come On In—

Free coffee and cake served at both Hamburg Inns.

HAMBURG INN #1
119 Iowa Avenue

Or

HAMBURG INN #2
214 North Linn

MONDAY OCT. 14

SIGN UP FOR T-SHIRT AND CLOCK... CHERRY COKE IN 32oz. TAKE HOM... CONTAINER ONLY 55¢. ANY FOUNTAIN DRINK IN A 32oz.... CONTAINER ONLY 55¢. HALF PRICE CUP OF COFFEE ALL DAY LONG!

...DAY OCT. 15

...FOR T-SHIRT AND CLOCK DRAWIN... ...OKE IN 32oz. TAKE HOME ...ER ONLY 55¢. ...NTAIN DRINK IN 32oz. TAKE HOM... ...ER ONLY 55¢. ...PLIMENTARY PIECE OF CARROT CAKE OR APPLE STRUESEL CAKE WITH

The 50s Time Capsule celebration took place in 1985; Fritz and Frances with their 25th Anniversary Hamburger Cake, 1973

Sometimes There's a Burger

Sometimes there's a burger,
& it's the right burger for its time and place.

Iowa beef, chunky & true,
home-ground & raised,
served up juicy with crunch
by the lovin' hands of your northside neighbor.

On a white bun that won't quit
soaking up the drippings & the
catsup & the mustard & that
would melt in your mouth if you would let it.

Sometimes there's a burger,
& it's the right burger for its time and place.

Hamburg Inn

Mike Lewis-Beck, 2008
60th Anniversary Poetry Contest

Dave at the 35th Anniversary Party, 1983

Ode on a Greasian Spoon

How do I love thee, Hamburg Inn Two
So much to list, let me begin to.

Thou pedigree of griddle and slow food
Galleons could sail on the java you've brewed

I love your belgian waffle and chocolate chip hot cake
I love your healthy garden salad and your decadent pie shake

Your tenderloins, burgers, chicken, fish, and omelet called Zadar
Thank heavens for little grills like yours and even your radar

After church crowds, catholic, jewish, muslim, pagan
Political players Obama to Reagan

Like panthers, the wait staff is both agile and swift
Like artists, the cooks show their culinary gift

I learned to like coffee on Hamburg Inn stools.
It's still a great place to recharge biofuels.

Sixty years you have graced your northside, number two, venue
Sixty more, grant us all please, to drool over the menu.

Dan Daly, an appreciative customer for at least 50 of your 60, 2008
60th Anniversary Poetry Contest

"We served over 500 burgers and met many guests who started coming to the Burg when my parents Fritz and Fran were just starting our 60 year tradition." [Dave speaking about the 60th Anniversary Free Lunch Day, August 25, 2008.] *Burg Diner Liner*, October 2008

55th Anniversary Celebration with the community, 2003 and again in 2008 for the 60th

Ode to Hamburg Inn

In counting the assets of Iowa City
Where connoisseurs and gourmets abide
There's one place you really should try
And you won't need a guide

For everyone here knows **Hamburg Inn!**
It's a place of wide renown
Because they have the best fresh ground burgers
Of any place in town

They've got catering and carry out
"Pie Shakes" and a "Grill on Wheels"
It's a place where smart folks meet
To talk and eat their meals

Like the economy you need a "Stimulus"
If only to ease your mind
And a good meal at **Hamburg Inn**
Is as good as you will find.

Roy Neumann, 2008
Chosen as the 60th Anniversary Poetry Contest Winner

"<u>Free</u> No Brainer Stress Ball When You Sign Up Today <u>for Royalty Rewards</u>"

Babaloon pays a visit

```
Hamburg Inn                                                                                              PAGE:    1
REPORT DATE: 03/06/2007                                                                          REPORT TIME: 14:06:28.28
-----------------------------------------------------------------------------------------------------------------------
                        ITEM SALES TREND ANALYSIS - ITEM BY ITEM - ITEMS WITH ZERO SALES EXCLUDED -
               FOR DATES FROM: Tues. Aug. 1, 2006  TO  Wed. Mar. 7, 2007    SHIFT: ENTIRE DAY    COST CENTER: ENTIRE HOUSE
                        |-------------- Period (218) --------------|  |--------- YTD Period Avg ( 49) ---------|
                              #Sold     Amount   Deletes    %Cat    %Tot         #Sold     Amount   Deletes    %Cat    %Tot
-----------------------------------------------------------------------------------------------------------------------
  1--Breakfast
    1--Omelets
         3    No Chz                                                                                          0.00    0.00
        31    Hash Browns                                                                                     0.00    0.00
        32    Home Fries                                                                                      0.00    0.00
       101    B.Y.O.O.                                                                                       17.71    3.38
       102    IOWA                                                                                           15.36    2.93
       103    DENVER                                                                                         12.13    2.32
       104    CALIFORNIA                                                                                      6.18    1.18
       105    FARMER'S                                                                                        8.55    1.63
       106    GARDEN FLOREN                                                                                   4.20    0.80
       107    ZADAR                                                                                           5.19    0.99
       108    GARDEN                                                                                          7.42    1.42
       109    FLORENTINE                                                                                      2.58    0.49
       110    RUEBEN                                                                                          1.37    0.26
       111    MEXI DELUXE                                                                                     3.62    0.69
       112    HULA                                                                                            1.57    0.30
       113    BENEDICT                                                                                        1.72    0.33
       114    MEXICAN                                                                                         1.63    0.31
       115    CHEF CLUB                                                                                       0.90    0.17
       116    CHICK CLUB                                                                                      2.68    0.51
       117    GOOSETOWN                                                                                       1.81    0.34
       178    HASHBROWNS                                                                                      4.35    0.83
       179    HOME FRIES                                                                                      0.89    0.17
       396    SICILIAN OM                                                                                     0.00    0.00
      1008    No CHOM                                                                                         0.16    0.03
      3001    No Toast            2227.00      0.00     23.00    0.00    0.00    2173.46      0.00    30.52   0.00    0.00
      3080    RONI                   0.00      0.00      1.00    0.00    0.00       4.96      0.00     0.00   0.00    0.00
            PRICED: Omelets     29556.00  140220.44    293.00  100.00   20.21   27097.40  128731.18  462.16 100.00   19.09
  2--Griddle
```

Hamburg Inn No. 2, another watercolor by server Niles Vaught

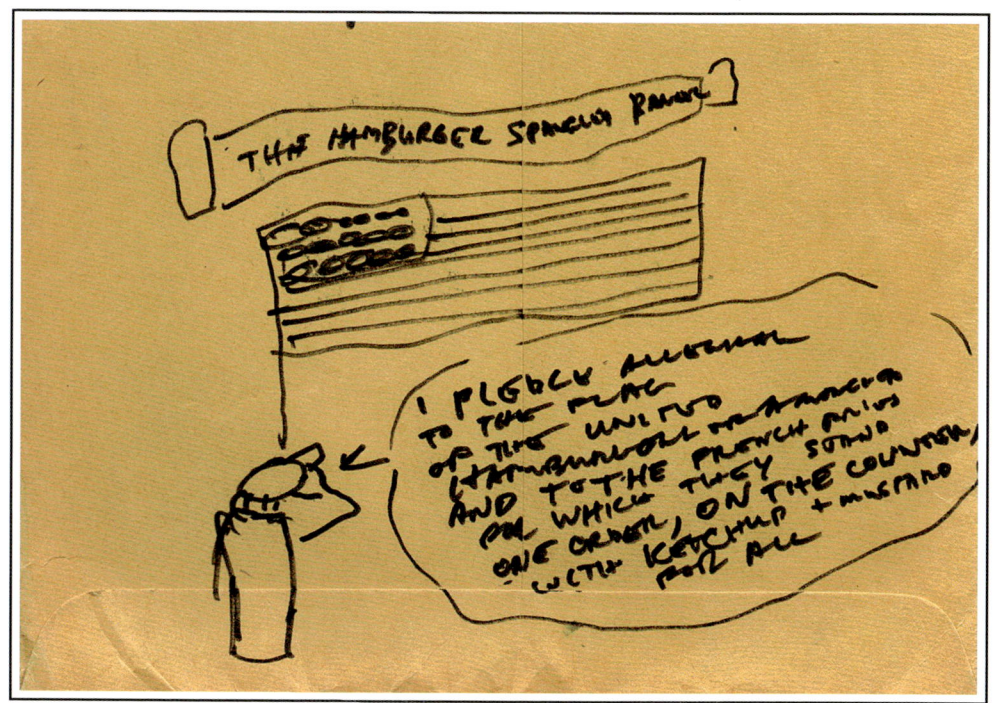

The Hamburger Spangled Banner

    I pledge allegiance
    to the flag
    of the United
    Hamburgers of America
    and to the French fries
    for which they stand
    one cream, on the counter,
    with ketchup & mustard for all.

Dave Morice, at the Hamburg Inn, 1970s

Morty Sklar

Caffeine, Nicotine, Meat & Warm Bodies Partaking of Nourishment

This ain't the Sheepshead
with its quiche, espresso, imported beer,
classical music, art major paintings, natural wood
decor, outdoor tables, hanging plants, exquisitely thin
slivers of rich pie at mod prices
and stylishly slow service...

and this ain't Simmy's with its
arty patron photo portraits, garbanzo bean burgers
and hot apple cider (10% juice, but swell glasses
& a sprinkle of cinnamon)...

    This is just a branch of the oldest eating establishment in the world--family. Hamburg Inn!

    Hey--I know I should have gone home, as usual,
after my two-mile jog and hour of calisthenics,
and made some stone-ground whole wheat flour
cornmeal buttermilk pancakes, topped with
honey and peaches, and brewed
some organic French roast coffee, but shit,
I'm a working man, and a man living alone, and I just wanted
someone to fix my meal, and besides, hamburgers are in
my genes--I can't deny my heritage. And besides, an
older woman in a dress is in my memory bank,
and even as an advanced human model as myself
draws on depth. And besides, poison is good for the

Nightfall— movie still

organic system, occasionally--hamburger & coffee
make the liver and kidneys work just like the muscles
and respiratory systems work when one labors them
with exercise.
And I like to ask someone, sometimes,
to pass the ketchup, or "Are you going to use
that ashtray?" And it's nice to leave the dishes
on the counter, and even leaving a tip
is a form of communication--if the service is good
or considerate.

    Hey--you wanna look good in your grandmother's dress
or your Jordache jeans, or your raggedy neo-hippie
cut-offs, headband and slouch? Go to the Sheepshead
or Simmy's. Someone there is gonna feel you fit,
or will hate you for being more different then they
    ...or maybe you just enjoy getting together with your friends
at a place you like. I'm no snob--I'm not saying
Hamburg Inn is the end-all & be-all. And I'll probably
see you at a $1.50 flick at the Bijou--which at a
Greenwich Village "art" theatre would be $6,
and then someone else could be talking about us
--someone who eats at Mr. Steak and goes to see
Superman IV or Star Wars VI.

    Nah, I'm not a snob--I like where I go.
I hope you like where you go too.
                                   July 1980

[While the Sheepshead and Simmy's have disappeared, the Hamburg Inn lives on.]

Hamburg Inn, 1970s and '80s
A Community Meeting Place By Any Other Name Is Still…

My first room in Iowa City was on South Dubuque, so for me Hamburg Inn was at the time the one on Iowa Avenue. I remember my eggs being scrambled soft the way I asked for them, and I won't forget Leanne who brought them to me. After a few visits, I was determined to ask her out but was disappointed to see a wedding ring on her hand. Was it the New Yorker in me or just your average guy who couldn't resist conveying my disappointment to her? —whereupon she confessed that she wore that ring, though divorced, to keep guys from hassling her. But this is about Hamburg Inn, not my love life, so…

My first hamburger at Hamburg Inn was at No. 2 (I mostly prepared meals at home and didn't eat meat often). When I ordered it medium rare, I sensed a pause in the waitress's pencil, and while waiting for my lunch to be prepared, I thought I heard only "hamburger" and "burger" being ordered, without adjectives, an odd thing to recall about forty years later, I guess, but as Patricia Grierson says in her poem "On The Details Of Life": "…But enough little things make all there is / Outside the Garden of Eden."

A sense of community such as I found in Iowa City can come to be taken for granted after awhile (though maybe not too easily if you've lived in New York City most of your life), but sometimes it hits you in the center of your being such as a day in October 1984 when I was headed to Hamburg Inn No. 2 (I almost wrote II, but referred to my Hamburg Inn T-shirts) when some guys waved and shouted at me from a pickup truck rounding a corner. My first thought was, I was being ribbed for the shoulder bag I was carrying. What else could it be? Then I heard "WAY T' GO!!" and saw a bunch of smiles. That day my photo had appeared on the front pages of the *Iowa City Press-Citizen* and the *Des Moines Register* with news of a small Iowa publisher's having been the first to bring out a book in the U.S.A. by little-known Czech poet, Jaroslav Seifert, who just won the Nobel Prize for Literature. My press, The Spirit That Moves Us Press, had published that book the year before, and just as thrilling as that news was (which got to me before the newspapers when at 7 a.m. that morning I was awakened by a phone call from Fritz, Bookseller to the Crown in Sweden, who ordered ten copies of Seifert's *The Casting Of Bells,* whereupon I exclaimed "WHY?!" and received the reply, "Oh, haven't you heard?—an author of yours, Jaroslav Seifert, just won the Nobel Prize.")—as thrilling as that was, just as thrilling was being cheered by my fellow townsmen in the pickup, and upon arriving at Hamburg Inn No. 2, receiving a standing ovation.

Maybe I've conveyed my feelings about Hamburg Inn No. 2 better in my 1980 poem, "Caffeine, Nicotine, Meat and Warm Bodies Partaking Of Nourishment," also in this book.

Looking forward to my wife's, Marcela's and my next visit to Iowa City and the Burg.

That Long and Winding Road Into Iowa City
Iowa City 1971 to 1989

My first trip up that long and winding road of North Dubuque Street off Interstate 80 into Iowa City in July 1971 is still fresh in my memory. Was it the tree-lined road and the fine summer day or was it my future unfolding? All I knew of Iowa City at the time was what Audrey Teeter had told me after the poetry festival in Allendale, Michigan, which had been my goal upon leaving New York City: "Iowa City is a nice place to live." She and her daughter were leading the way. My Honda 305cc Dream wasn't a travel bike, but held-up pretty good, my having purchased the year-old model assembled brand new out of the box for $695.

    At The Mill, where Audrey first took me, I saw some familiar faces, one of whom was a guy at the poetry festival who'd come up to me after I'd read at the open reading and said, "I was falling asleep, until your poem 'Bed' woke me. It was Allan Kornblum, poet and editor/publisher of *Toothpaste* magazine and the subsequent and current Coffee House Press, who six years later published my first collection from his letterpress, The Toothpaste Press, *The Night We Stood Up For Our Rights: Poems 1969–1975*. Among others I recognized were Darrell Gray, poet and editor/publisher of *Suction* magazine; Dave Morice, poet and editor/publisher of *Gum* magazine, as well as writer of marathon poems and the persona of Dr. Alphabet; George Mattingly, poet and editor/publisher of Blue Wind Press; Anselm Hollo, poet, translator and teacher; and others, all of whom were part of a community of poets and "little-maggers" outside the realm of the University and its Writer's Workshop that had become a different animal from the one that Paul Engle established, and a group who became known as The Actualists, named as such by Darrell Gray with whom I co-edited *The Actualist Anthology*, published from my The Spirit That Moves Us Press six years later, the contributors being Allan Kornblum, Cinda Kornblum, Chuck Miller, Anselm Hollo, John Batki, Jim Mulac, David Hilton, Sheila Heldenbrand, Steve Toth, George Mattingly, Dave Morice, John Sjoberg, and Darrell and me, as well as sketches of the poets and the book design by Pat Dooley.

    I didn't exactly fall right in with these guys and gals, not being used to hanging-out, but was made to feel welcome by their general openness and warmth, and of course their enjoyment of what they were doing was contagious. It helped that my own poetry was enjoyed by them. An early turning point for me was Dave Morice's asking if he could see more of my work after I'd submitted some to his and others' mags, and his laughing while reading through some unsubmitted poems. He asked why he hadn't seen the ones that caused him to laugh, and I said "Well, they're not my serious ones; I want to be taken seriously as a poet," whereupon Dave said "Humor is serious, too."

The first collating party I joined was for a new issue of *Toothpaste*, an 8 1/2 x 14 stapled-on-the-side mimeographed poetry mag assembled at the apartment of its editor/publisher Allan Kornblum and his wife-to-be Cinda. In 1975, I put out the first issue of *The Spirit That Moves Us* magazine, named for what my mother used to say, "If the spirit moves you, do it." In 5 1/2 x 8 1/2 format, I mimeographed the text from electronically cut stencils and had the cover printed offset with a duotone of my grandmother holding year-old me to her bosom with one arm. Meanwhile, our community of poets and little-maggers thrived with readings at Epstein's Books, The Sanctuary Tavern, Actualist Conventions, and elsewhere. The Sanctuary readings were hosted by Jim Mulac, the last of this community whom I'd come to know, at whose Jim's Used Books and Records on South Dubuque frequent readings occurred by Actualists as well as participants from around the world who were attending the International Writing Program, and visitors from out-of-town. Jim also edited with me the first volume of The Spirit That Moves Us Press's Editor's Choice series, the 500-page Literature and Graphics from the U.S. Small Press, 1965–1977, published in 1980 and inspired by the Pushcart Prize.

Iowa City for me was where I completed my adolescence, which had begun with social withdrawal, crime, drug addiction, dishonorable discharge from the 82nd Airborne (years later changed to honorable) after serving time in the disciplinary barracks, and segued to helping to establish the Phoenix House Therapeutic Community for drug abuse in 1966, then graduating from it in 1969, meeting my first true love and seeing her depart the city not long after, then working a nine-to-five and taking my first poetry workshop, with Isabella Gardner, after writing with no contact with other poets or readings for many years, then heading-out to the first National Poetry Festival in July 1971, and at age thirty-six becoming a social being who dated women and got a life. I returned to the city of my birth in 1989 when my mother became ill. Previous to Iowa City, my biggest accomplishment was attaining a state that most people were already in—drug-free. I still mention it, the way World War II veterans still meet, and out of reverence for having survived, and having been taken to The City of my Dreams.

Morty Sklar, July 2011

Morty Sklar was one of the founding members of the Actualist Poetry movement and began his press, The Spirit That Moves Us Press, in 1975 while living in Iowa City. The press has brought out many titles including the *Actualist Anthology*. Two of his short essays highlight the Hamburg Inn of the 70s and the beginnings of the Actualist Poetry Movement.

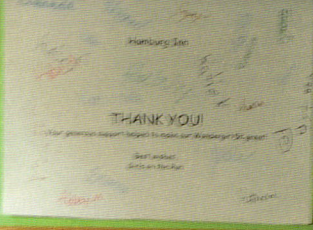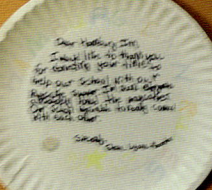

Hope Edelman

The mugs made all the difference. White and ceramic, chunky and substantial, they were the kind of mugs that said, "Hot coffee, serious coffee. Right here. Right now." In 1992 you could find similar mugs at The Great Midwestern coffeehouse on Washington Street, but you also ran the risk of seeing your recently ex-boyfriend there with his shockingly new girlfriend. So not always the best idea. The Cottage on Linn Street was another option but it closed after lunch. The Hamburg Inn was a straight shot down Market Street from the ancient blue-brick building where I lived so the Burg became my destination when I needed someplace outside the house to work. The writers didn't go there, and you could eat your egg salad sandwich without interruption and pretend that the guy you'd thought you'd loved didn't have a shockingly new girlfriend, or that he didn't even exist.

Plus, those mugs.

This was long before wifi, even before laptops. Writers in coffee shops still had to use paper, a method that seems both quaintly archaic and vaguely ridiculous now. I would sit at the side tables at the Hamburg Inn, back against the wall, and sketch out personal essays on yellow legal pads with black fine-tip pens. I could nurse a thick white mug of coffee for well more than an hour before any of the wait staff noticed I was still there. Sometimes slow service had its benefits. If I needed to procrastinate I brought my bills and paid them at the table. Or I read books and highlighted them with fat yellow markers. Then I walked the five blocks home and finished the night writing on an IBM desktop with two floppy drives.

The Nonfiction Writing Program was a fledging program back then, very much in the shadow of the Writer's Workshop, and Creative Nonfiction still a genre in search of a definition. "Creative Nonfiction? Isn't that an oxymoron?" my Workshop friends would ask. The NWP hadn't yet been accredited for an MFA; instead we all got something called an MA/W in English, though nobody really knew what that meant. Not that it mattered. We wanted to write about events that had really happened and the impressions they'd made on us. That's what we were there for. We just wrote.

In the spring of 1992 I sold a book proposal for a nonfiction book about early mother loss and its lifelong effects on women. My mother had died of cancer when I was seventeen and I'd been looking for a book on the subject for the past ten years. Finally I decided to write it myself, working on the proposal and sample chapter at the side tables in the Burg on and off for eight months. The sale meant…well, it meant everything. It meant I could pay my final semester's tuition and graduate on time, that I could move to New York with two of my Workshop friends, and that I could support myself as a writer for at least the coming year.

Thank you notes left by Horace Mann students, after the Burg did their school pancake supper

My last weekend in Iowa City—bicycle sold, houseplants relocated, refrigerator emptied and scrubbed clean—I ate a final breakfast at the Hamburg Inn. The side tables were all taken on a Sunday morning so I sat at the counter instead. The waiter placed a thick white mug of coffee in front of me. I looked at it as if I were saying goodbye to an old friend.

Midway through my omelette I felt another customer's eyes on me. Two stools away a man was staring at me with an expression of pure sadness and longing. He was middle-aged, shirtsleeves and jeans, could have used a shave. The staring went on for five minutes or more. I'll be honest: it was creepy. I finished my breakfast and hurried to pay the bill.

Standing at the cash register, I felt a tapping on my shoulder. It was him.

"I'm sorry," he said. "I hope I didn't bother you. But ten years ago I lost my daughter and you look so much like she'd look as an adult. Thank you for letting me look at you."

I hadn't seen that one coming. And I believed him. Anyone who's lost a loved one knows how grief can make you wish for things that aren't there and can never be. I would think of this man often in the coming year, every time a motherless woman told me a story about seeing her mother's face in a crowded shopping mall, or following a stranger for half an hour on a city street just to feel, even if only for a short while, that she was in the presence of the person she most wanted to be with. I would sit in living rooms in New York City and cafes in San Francisco and backyards in Chicago suburbs and listen to these stories, and they'd all transport me back to Iowa City, onto a round stool at the counter of the Hamburg Inn, letting a stranger stare at me for a few minutes longer to believe in something he couldn't otherwise have.

"It's all right," I told the man at the cash register. "I understand. Really."

A few hours later I got into the U-Haul with two fiction writers from the Workshop and started heading east on I-80. It wasn't the kind of farewell from Iowa City I might have written for myself, but it was a better sendoff than I could have imagined.

Hope Edelman is the author of the international bestseller Motherless Daughters and four other nonfiction books. She lives in Topanga Canyon, California, where she teaches at Antioch University-LA and spends every summer back in Iowa City.

Dawn, breakfast, winter

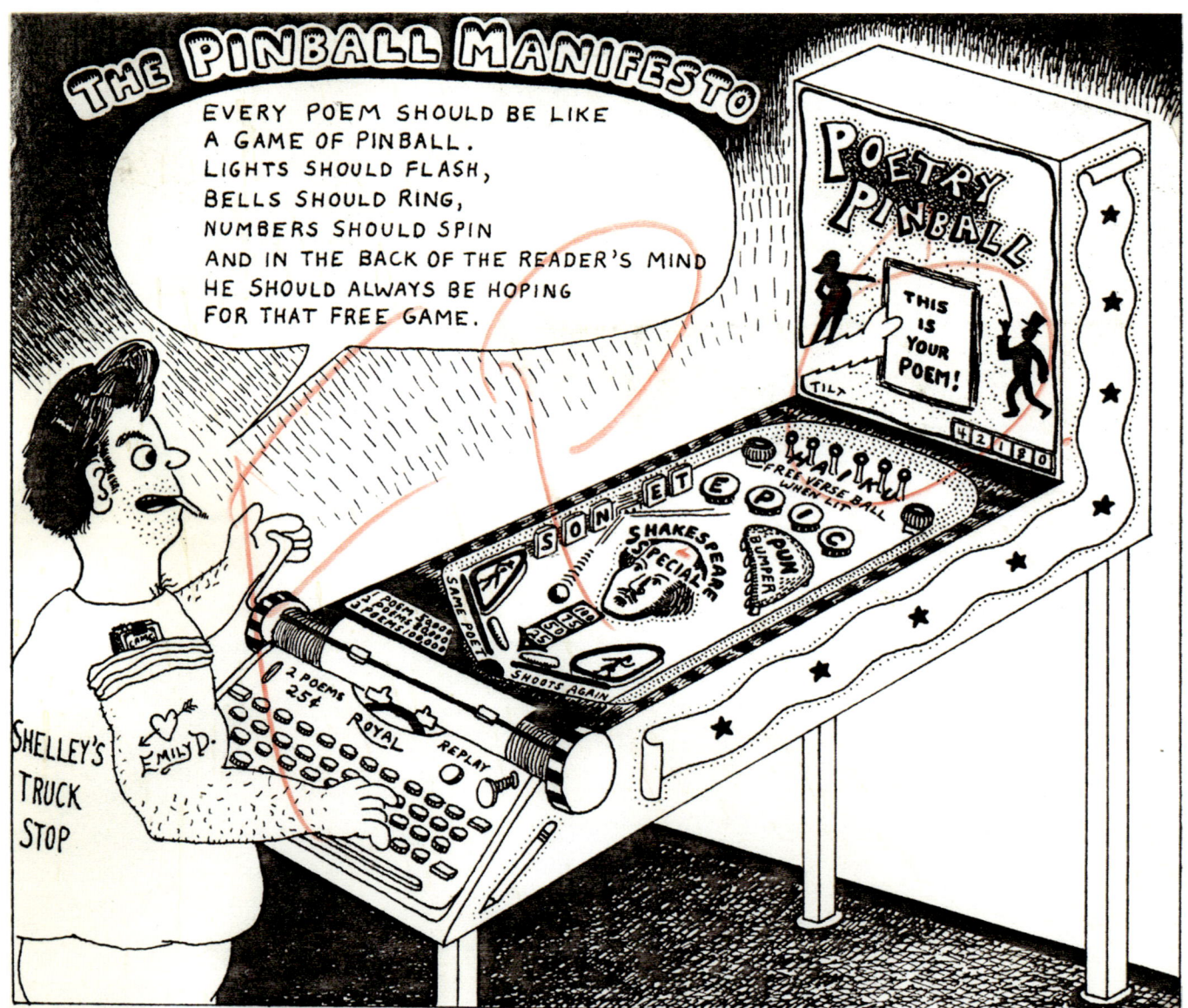

Dave Morice's drawing, "The Pinball Manifesto" refers to the Satin Doll pinball machine in the front of the diner in the 1970s

Asked what were the best of times for him, Dave Panther named two: working in partnership with his brother Mike and the Coffee Bean Caucus'. The first Coffee Bean Caucus began on January 7, 2004, preceding the Iowa Caucus on the 19th. But before coffee beans were used, voting was done with ketchup:

Hamburg Inn is running a Coffee Bean Poll. Patrons get a coffee bean with each purchase of food. When paying the check, they drop the coffee bean into one of three presidential bowls—one for Bush, the other for Kerry. Third is The Vinegar Bowl, where patrons drop their coffee bean if they are sour on both candidates…Before the Coffee Bean Poll, the owner staged Ketchup Wars. Customers had their choice of two bottles of ketchup to squirt on their fries. One bottle was labeled 'W' ketchup, for those in favor of a second term for you-know-who. The other was Heinz 57 ketchup. That needs no explanation, either. There was a fuss over Ketchup Wars. "Some customers got riled, saying the political process was too serious a thing to involve ketchup. So we substituted our Coffee Bean Poll for the ketchup. Actually, the bean poll is more definitive," David says. Wundram, *Quad-City Times,* October 2004

Asked if the dialogue ever escalates in one of the most polarized elections in recent memory, the owner cited a marketing ploy gone awry. After placing both Heinz and 'W' ketchup bottles on each table in what was tabbed the 'Ketchup Wars,' he saw some unfavorable results. "After awhile, all that was left were the 'W' bottles, and people were very upset that we would put those out there… A row of clear Mason jars sitting on a window ledge are filled with coffee beans in the first annual 'bean ballot poll." Kerr, *The Daily Iowan,* November 2004

Some Noteworthy Visitors

President Bill Clinton
President Barack Obama
President Ronald Reagan
Vice President Joe Biden
Governor Terry Branstad
Governor Chet Culver
Governor Howard Dean
Governor Mitt Romney
Governor Tom Vilsack & Christie Vilsack
Senator Chris Dodd
Senator John Edwards & Elizabeth Edwards
Senator Tom Harkin
Senator Dennis Kucinich
Senator John McCain
Senator Bill Richardson
Congressman Jim Leach
Congressman Dave Loebsack
Congresswoman Mary Mascher
General Wesley Clark
Doctor Patch Adams
Garrison Keilor, author, radio personality
Rob Reiner, director
John Waters, director
Rosanne Barr & Tom Arnold, actors
Martin Sheen, actor, 'President Jed Bartlett' in West Wing
Mary Steenburgen & Ted Danson, actors
Tucker Carlson of CNN's Crossfire
John Roberts of CNN's American Morning
Patrick Buchanan
Lovin' Spoonful, rock band

"I had a great omelet at the Hamburg Inn."

Opening line of Barack Obama's Earth Day speech at the University of Iowa to a crowd of 10.000, April 22, 2007

Clinton made sure to greet each of about 12 diners before taking his seat at a booth near his photo on the wall …. "This is really great," he [Dave Panther] said. "He's sitting in the same place he sat last time…People kept streaming in and out of the diner during Clinton's visit." Fiegen, *Iowa City Press-Citizen,* November 2007

Clinton remembered his first visit, now the Clinton table. His autograph is framed nearby.

The first of President Bill Clinton's two stops at the Hamburg Inn, here meeting the waitstaff: Biswamit Dwibedy and Rae Ann Nordmeyer in 2003

Vote Today
Vote Tomorrow
Hamburg Inn's Coffee Bean Caucus
One Bean One Vote

The Burg will be holding it's Coffee Bean Caucus from the 7th to 18th of Janurary to help kick off Iowa's Official Caucus on Monday the 19th.

Vote for your favorite Candidate everytime you dine with us. All the Democatic Presidential Candidates plus President Bush each have a Mason Jar Ballot Box to cast your Bean!
Get your bean from the Staff or at the Register.

General Wesley Clark

Actors Martin Sheen and Rob Reiner campaigning for Howard Dean

Governor Howard Dean

Senator John Edwards

"This has been something else," Panther said. [John] Edwards came to speak at the cafe in late August, and hundreds of people packed inside and spilled out onto the sidewalk. "That was the biggest event we ever had…" Fiegen, *Iowa City Press-Citizen,* December 2007

Using garden variety canning jars, one labeled for each candidate running for president (with one jar labeled 'I don't care'), customers vote, via coffee bean, for their favorite candidate... some local customers vote several times a day. The only rule: Decaffeinated beans are not allowed. Meyer, *AAA Living,* January/February 2008

Hamburg Inn No.2 Inc.
Coffee Bean Caucus
Vote Tally

Kucinich	**Total** 546	**%** 17.7
Dean	**Total** 654	**%** 21.2
Moseley Braun	**Total** 70	2.3
Clark	**Total** 219	**%** 7.1
Kerry	**Total** 427	**%** 13.8
Gephardt	**Total** 131	**%** 4.2
Edwards	**Total** 265	**%** 8.6
Lieberman	**Total** 33	**%** 1.1
Sharpton	**Total** 74	**%** 2.4
Bush	**Total** 379	**%** 12.3
Undecided	**Total** 286	**%** 9.3
Total Vote	**Total** 3084	**%** 100

In an impromptu breakfast stop, former President Clinton dined ....on home fries and a Swiss cheese, tomato and green pepper omelet, then plunked down a coffee bean for Hillary Clinton. "I was glad to put a bean in...." Binegar, *Cedar Rapids Gazette,* November 2007

Senator Dennis Kucinich visited on January 18, 2004, seen here with a supporter

Senator Chris Dodd

Governor Mitt Romney and Mrs. Romney

Senator John McCain with the Dan Gables

Vice President Joe Biden

[Joe] Biden stopped at the restaurant, 214 N. Linn St., to participate in its traditional coffee bean caucus and to pitch his ideas to locals as they ate syrup-soaked pancakes and scrambled eggs. "I'm a U.S. senator, I'm accustomed to not being taken seriously, so continue to eat," he joked to the packed restaurant. Binegar, *Cedar Rapids Gazette,* August 2007

...Coffee Bean Caucuses [are] hosted during the primaries. Three weeks before the election, waiters leave coffee beans on the tables, opening the forum for people to talk about the candidates and the issues. With a row of glass jars on the front counter, customers place their coffee bean vote for a candidate when they make a decision. At the end of three weeks, managers count the beans to determine the winner..... By initiating discourse, the inn did its part in getting people involved in the process. "We serve a side order of politics here," he [Manager Steve Fugate] said. Richter, *The Hawk Eye*, January 2005

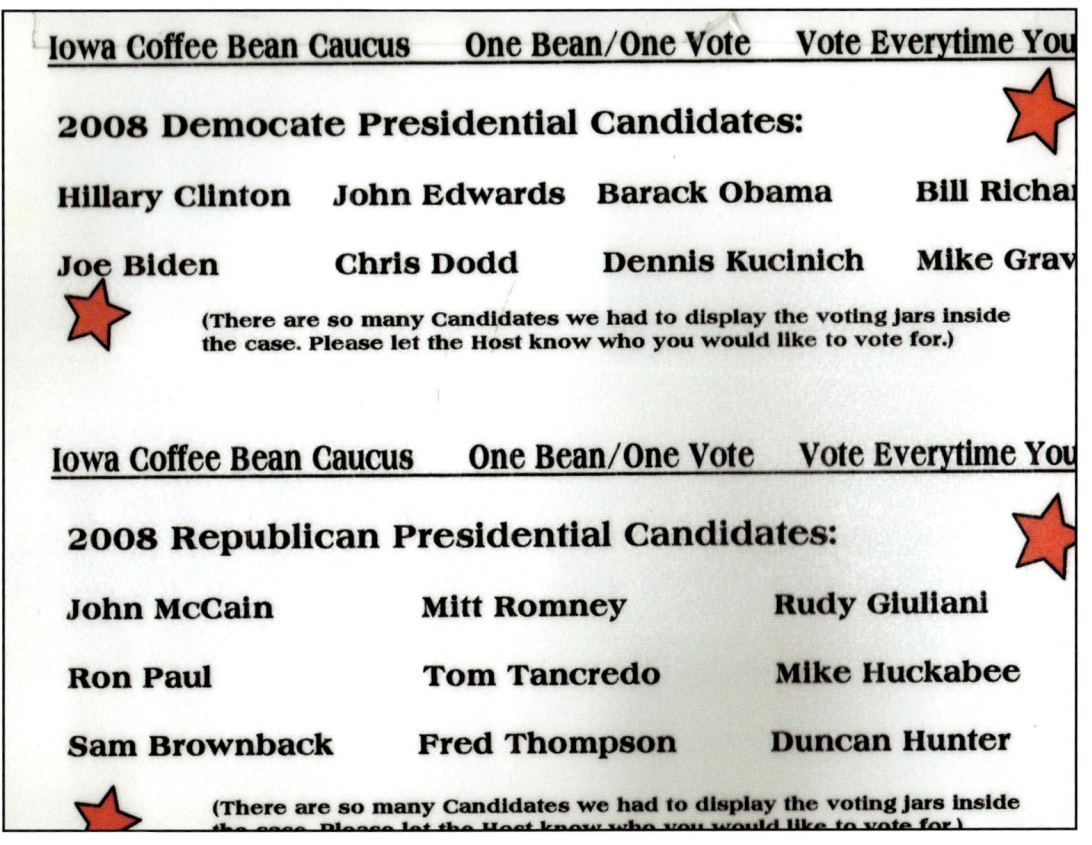

On Iowa's caucus day, January 3, 2008: Obama got 1,733 beans; Hillary-830, Edwards-445, Ron Paul-132 beans for 3140 + votes vs. 3084 in 2004, when Dean won with 654 beans, Kucinich came in 2nd with 546 beans.

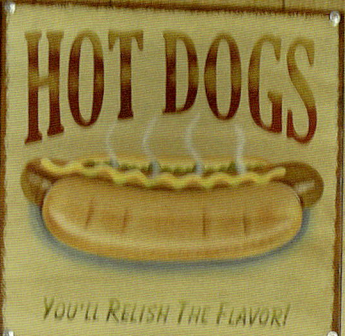

On Wednesday, CNN commandeered one corner, flooding the space with cameras and lights. The spotlight was on as Panther emptied the jars to count votes. CNN 'American Morning' anchor John Roberts said he's covered elections, but he's never experienced anything quite like the Hamburg's bean poll. Binegar, *Cedar Rapids Gazette,* December 2008

What the candidates ate:

Senator Barack Obama had an Iowa omelet with sweet potato pancakes, April 22, 2007

President Bill Clinton ordered a chocolate shake and took some hamburgers to go, March 27, 2003

President Bill Clinton had home fries and a Swiss cheese, tomato and green pepper omelet, November 27, 2007

President Ronald Reagan ordered Dutch apple pie and meatloaf, August 25, 2007

Senator Dennis Kucinich loved the vegetarian chili, January 15, 2004

Senator John Edwards had the Iowa Breakfast, August 17, 2007

Senator John McCain had a milkshake, May 8, 2007

General Wesley Clark had an egg-white garden omelet, September 20, 2003

Patrick Buchanan ordered a double cheeseburger and fries, 1999

"The restaurant always sends the candidates off with a bag of burgers to enjoy on the road." Demas, 2004

Autographed CNN poster, 2008

Jean Lloyd-Jones

It was the place to go for my teenage son and his friends in the '70's, so I thought only kids hung out at Hamburg Inn. The first time I set foot in the place was when University President Hunter Rawlings invited Johnson County legislators to breakfast one morning. It was a surprise to me to see students and homeless people, some of whom may have been there much of the night, alongside business and political folks.

Only then did I learn that it was a legendary stop on the campaign trail, where presidents and candidates could schmooze with voters and customers got to vote for their favorite candidate by dropping coffee beans into bottles. After that, I made it a point to schedule CIVIC's* international visitors there for lunch when time permitted.

Once Jim McPherson met with an Indonesian poet for lunch, and afterwards conducted him to the Writers' Workshop to observe a class. Another time a group of European political leaders enjoyed Bison Burgers and happily voted for the most conservative political candidate in the race. Many times I have enjoyed lunch there with friends, and cast my own votes.

Hamburg Inn is a treasured part of the Iowa City landscape and a key component of the Northside Literary District. I hope it will continue to be a vital part of the community for decades to come.

*Council for International Visitors to Iowa Cities

Jean Lloyd-Jones served in the Iowa Legislature for 16 years (eight in the House and eight in the Senate) from 1979-1995. She ran unsuccessfully for the U.S. Senate in 1992.

Mary Mascher

What do Barack Obama, Ronald Reagan, Bill Clinton, Wesley Clark, Dennis Kucinich, Howard Dean, and Pat Buchanan all have in common? They all have visited the Hamburg Inn in the course of their political campaigns. Few restaurants in the River City can boast of hosting some of the most notable presidents and presidential candidates in the country but the Hamburg Inn has proudly hosted many. Add to the list of visitors, Elizabeth Edwards, Rob Reiner, Martin Sheen, and Patch Adams and you can see why this local restaurant has become the hub of political discussions and debates. Over the years Dave Panther has been a gracious host to democratic and republican candidates alike. In 2004 he launched the Coffee-bean Poll, in which each guest is given a coffee bean to place in the jar of his/her candidate. In 2004 Howard Dean was the winner of the "Bean Poll" and in 2008 Barack Obama was the overwhelming favorite. The Hamburg Inn was featured on the "King Corn" episode of the TV show, The West Wing and was the filming location for the comedy film, Zadar! Cow From Hell". But it is not only national candidates who seek to meet the public at this popular local restaurant, state and local candidates also flock to the Hamburg Inn to meet with voters. Recently former Governor Chet Culver chose this gathering spot to meet with Iowans on his farewell tour across the state.

As a state legislator, I have had the privilege of being a Hamburg Inn customer for over 40 years. While attending the University of Iowa, I was a frequent visitor at the Hamburg Inn No. 1 on Iowa Ave. It was a great location to meet friends for lunch or to stop for a quick bite between classes. I mourned its closing but was heartened to know that the Linn Street location would continue to provide the same quality service and food as the downtown location. I know I share my love of the Hamburg Inn with many Iowans and appreciate the warm atmosphere and sense of community you experience every time you walk in the door. Few restaurants can boast of such a unique role in the history of politics in our state. The Hamburg Inn is a landmark in that right but more importantly it is a great place to eat and gather with family and friends.

Mary Mascher is a state legislator from Iowa City who represents Iowa House District #77. Mascher was elected to the Iowa House in 1994 and serves on the education, human resources, and state government committees. She is an assistant leader in the House Democratic Caucus.

Caucus season 2011

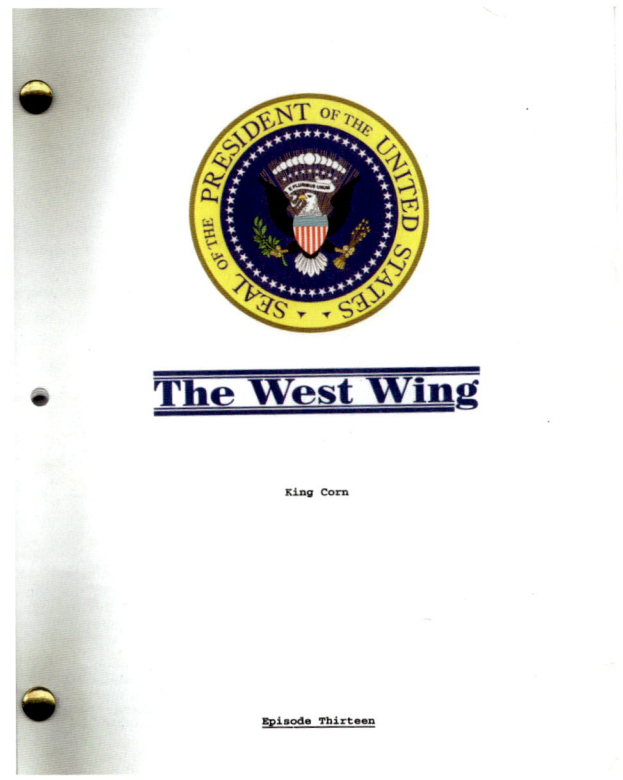

After their visit to the Burg on January 14, 2004, the actors Martin Sheen and Rob Reiner took the idea of the Coffee Bean Caucus back to the set of NBC's *The West Wing*. Episode 13 was based on what they'd observed in Iowa City. About a year later, 'King Corn' aired on national television and was viewed on a 52" screen set up in the diner. Patrons were invited to vote for the fictional candidates a few days before the screening.

[Alan Alda portrays a fictional GOP presidential candidate, Senator Arnold Vinick, and got 54 beans vs. Jimmy Smits as Representative Matthew Santos—last place in show but first at Burg with 214 beans; VP candidate Gary Coleman got 33 beans.] As the votes are cast on television for the fictional candidates, visitors to the real-life restaurant will have the opportunity to vote for the characters during a viewing party. Panther said it would start about 30 minutes before the show begins at 8 p.m. Pracht, *Iowa City Press-Citizen*, January 2005

The West Wing: 'King Corn' Episode

The crowd cheered at each mention of the restaurant [during the January 26th viewing]. Presidential candidates portrayed by Alan Alda and Jimmy Smits stopped at the recreated Hamburg Inn No. 2, which was filmed inside a Pasadena, CA, restaurant....In the show, aides drank from the restaurant's mugs while they studied the number of coffee beans inside jars that were part of the coffee bean caucus for which the restaurant became famous during last year's Iowa Caucuses.

Hamburg Inn owner Dave Panther was pleased to see the shot of his restaurant's logo on national television. "They got a shot of the logo, the restaurant was in a brick building, they used the mugs we sent them," Panther said. "We got two verbal mentions, a good explanation of the coffee bean caucus. It was good." Kucharski, *Cedar Rapids Gazette,* January 2005

Each time the actors walked by a red brick building, the sounds of clattering forks and balloon bursts seemed to stop as patrons craned their necks for a clear view of the 52-inch TV. Some patrons even screamed at the TV, "Go back and eat breakfast!" Bello, *Iowa City Press-Citizen,* January 2005

Television script and signed T-shirt from West Wing crew

John Deeth

I've always thought Hillary Clinton's fatal mistake in the Iowa Caucuses was skipping out on the Hamburg Inn. Bill stopped by, sure. The Big Dog had been there before, in 2003, and wasn't going to miss out on a great meal.

But Hillary was never comfortable with the chat and chew aspects of the Iowa caucuses, and never stopped by.

Barack Obama did, even though it was just for a quick unannounced shake before his massive Earth Day 2007 rally. John McCain did, accompanied by wrestling legend Dan Gable.

John Edwards sort of did. But like so many things with Edwards, there was a touch of the artificial, as he never actually set foot in the door. The pre-event crowd got so large that it spilled out onto and into Linn Street, and Edwards spoke from a stepladder at the door of his campaign bus.

It was a dramatic moment, and by accident a photo of the event got me the unearned honor of a photo on the Hamburg's wall. (You have to look really close.) But it's wasn't in essence a Hamburg Inn moment. It was a rally that happened to be in front of the Hamburg Inn.

For my money, no one did a better Hamburg Inn event than Joe Biden. The other reporters I worked with juggled other assignments with some reluctance: "Do I HAVE to go cover Bill Clinton I saw him LAST week?" Yes, we Iowans are that spoiled.

But we always hustled to try to get the Biden assignment, even though he was an asterisk in the year of the stars. It was like covering a great band that changed its set list every night: you never knew what you were going to hear but you knew it would rock.

Owner Dave Panther started to introduce the senator at the 7:30 AM with some biography, but Biden pshawed the plaudits: "I'm Joe Biden."

Biden began speaking literally next to me, sitting with good luck at the Bill Clinton table. I reached around him and placed my audio recorder on the lunch counter in front of him. Biden reached down and carefully positioned my recorder about 2 inches away from where I'd set it.

Candidate Terry Branstad campaigning at the Burg, February 2010

Biden strolled back and forth behind the counter, at arms length from diners, occasionally using the restaurant accoutrements as props. "If you're moving two trillion dollars of the economy from here to here," he said of health care, "there's going to be winners and losers." Biden illustrated the shifting trillions by picking up a sugar shaker and moving it from his right to his left. He emphasized one statement by tapping a salt shaker like a gavel.

The speech was short, the questions were many, and the answers extended. Biden took roughly a half dozen questions and expounded in depth on each, for as long as ten minutes a question, more time than he was getting in entire debates.

At one point, Biden noticed a small knot of three or four people waiting outside the front door and interrupted his remarks to urge them to come on in. A person near the inner door opened it, and the folks outside opened the outer door and entered. The crowd near the door shifted, but not much, to accommodate the new arrivals. It was the kind of moment that makes every other state except New Hampshire jealous.

So many other stories and memories, with a few standing out:

- Terry McAuliffe trying to flirt with my wife ("sure she's not your daughter?") while having a low key dinner and working the crowd with Leonard Boswell for Hillary Clinton.

- An awkward chat between two former Democratic congressional colleagues: David Bonior, managing the John Edwards campaign, and a slightly paranoid Cynthia McKinney, who'd bolted the party to run for president as a Green.

- Funny off the record stories from Chris Dodd in the dying days of his long shot campaign.

If you want to attend a Hamburg Inn political event here's my advice:

- Show up early. Tables are always at a premium at the Burg – if it were bigger, it wouldn't be the same. And you run the risk of interlopers. A 2003 Howard Dean campaign event with Rob Reiner and The West Wing's own Martin Sheen was marred by an advance invasion by team Dennis Kucinich (who had a special, inexplicable hostility to Dean).

- Beware of the Heisenberg Effect. In science, the Heisenberg effect, or "observer effect," describes a phenomenon in which the observation or measurement of an event changes the very nature of the event. For example, attaching a meter to an electrical circuit to measure the current inherently changes that current. Or, in presidential politics, a candidate visiting a diner changes the nature of the diner.

- Take care of your wait staff. The hoopla and excitement may be fun for you, but remember someone is depending on your table for making a living that shift. It's OK to get just coffee if you tip really, really well, but why would you want to settle for just that?

- If you're the incumbent president, show up. It's the one missing item on the Dave Panther Bucket List. He's had two formers and one future, but never an incumbent.

John Deeth is a *Des Moines Register* guest blogger who has been featured in publications ranging from the Drudge Report to the Huffington Post. His past affiliations include WSUI radio (NPR) and Iowa Independent. Deeth and his trademark raspberry beret were a frequent presence on the 2007 Iowa caucus scene. Deeth is also a political activist in Johnson County and the Democratic Party, and ran for the Iowa legislature in 1996.

A Davenport couple visiting the city

Dick Vitosh has the record for longest-standing regular

Roseanne and Tom actually did visit

Gary Wickenkamp, another regular for the last 5-6 years

Talia and Luke working a cross-word puzzle on late afternoon break

A visit from Mrs. United States

John Waters

Patch Adams for Kucinich, January 2004

Dave and Roma Panther having lunch

John Deeth covering the Branstad stop

Garrison Keilor

Marvin and Dorothy Bell

Laurel Snyder

Smiley (Gary Lee Bloare) showing off his button collection

Karen Kubby

Memories of Hamburg Inn

Memories. That is the essence of Hamburg Inn. Memories. The Burg is an anchor for the Northside Marketplace commercial area. It has created great memories for me personally and for the community.

My mother created special times for each of her daughters. Each girl would go out to lunch with just mom. We loved to go to Hamburg Inn #1 on Iowa Avenue. We loved the burgers and the fries.

Our family moved away from Iowa City in 1973 and I returned in 1978. Going to the Hamburg Inn was part of that return. I never worked at Hamburg Inn, although I know a lot of people who have worked at this iconic local business. Shortly after I returned to Iowa City to go to the University of Iowa, I became a vegetarian. There was still plenty for me to choose from at the Burg. It was a great shift when the Burg began offering a black bean burger. Now I could go out for a burger and fries again! My favorite is the Swiss Mushroom burger with a black bean patty and super crispy fries. I haven't been to the Burg lately. I have to admit that just writing this has me salivating a bit and will likely get me back to the Burg sooner rather than later. That's great, because I have a birthday coupon and can get more reward points for my indulgence.

Being able to have breakfast all day long is important in a college town. People are doing all kinds of things at all hours. Whether it's a leisurely Sunday afternoon or a late night snack after a movie or bar closing time, being able to order hash browns with veggies or a sweet potato pancake any time you want is a great community service.

Hamburg Inn also has created great memories community and nationwide. The tongue in cheek and serious art of campaigning through the Coffee Bean Caucus has made the Burg a must stop for any serious politician. Candidates of all persuasions seek to host an event at the Burg and many do. The space is perfect, because the photo opt will likely show an overcrowded space, as it isn't that big in the first place. It's also a great boost for business so it's a perfect part of the Burg's business plan. People all over the country know about the Burg because of the Coffee Bean Caucus, so when they come to Iowa City to visit, the Burg is at the top of the list for a meal and a that's so Iowa City experience.

Hamburg Inn, thanks for all the memories you have created for generations of people that live, work, go to school and pass through Iowa City. There are generations of memories yet to create.

Ajax doing prep work

Karen Kubby is President of Kubby Gyrls, Inc. and the co-owner of Beadology Iowa, a downtown Iowa City retail bead store offering finished jewelry, beads, and instruction. The store philosophy has a focus on customer service, social responsibility and community involvement. She is the Grant Writer and former Executive Director of the Emma Goldman Clinic, a 38-year old feminist non-profit reproductive health care facility located in Iowa City. She is an experienced community activist and volunteer since 1979, raising money for non-profit organizations, social change causes and political campaigns. Karen served her community as an appointed member of the ad-hoc Human Rights Commission in 1984 and the Committee on Community Needs (now Housing and Community Development Commission) from 1984 to 1999. She served as an elected city council member from 1989 to 2000.

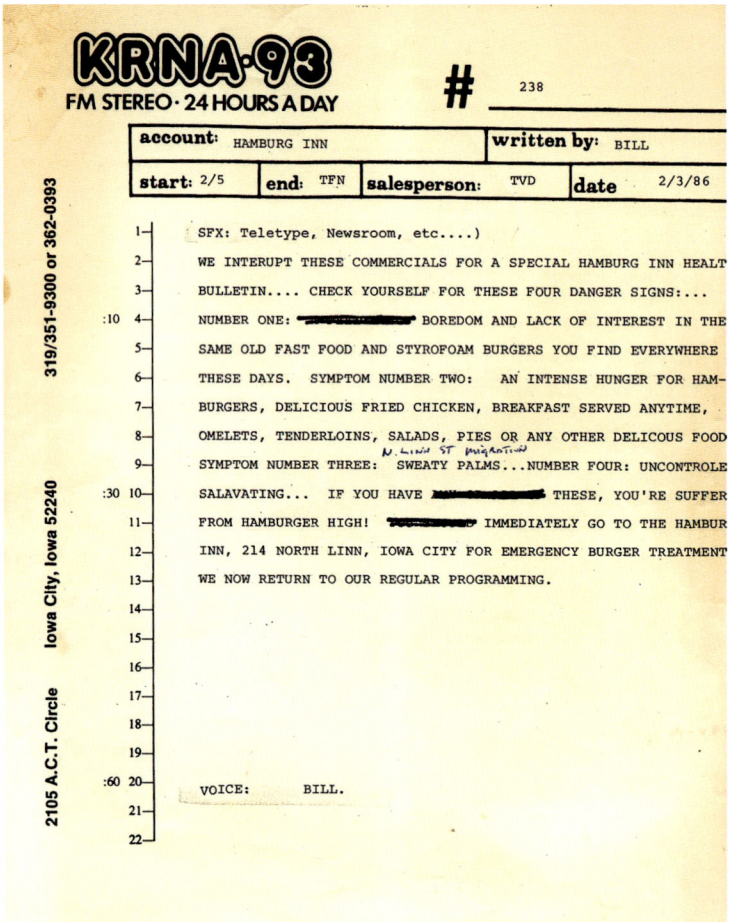

Brittany Burggraaf's downstairs wall mural was commissioned by the Hamburg Inn

Steve Toth

TABULA RASA

As the waitress
    clears our table
    wiping everything clean
we are getting a fresh start
    as if this were the first
    meal ever served in this place

These are the nights when
    life seems to be coming in
    like rock & roll music
& being open
    to being transported
    we have joined the dance

Steve Toth was born in northern Minnesota not far from the source of the Mississippi. Grew up in Eastern Iowa on the banks on that same river. Went to poetry school at the University of Iowa. With some friends went on to found the Actualist poetry movement. Met Sheila, fell in love and married. Later we moved to Los Angeles and now living where the Pacific Ocean, Coastal mountains and redwood forest all come together in extreme Northwestern California.

Chris and Chris

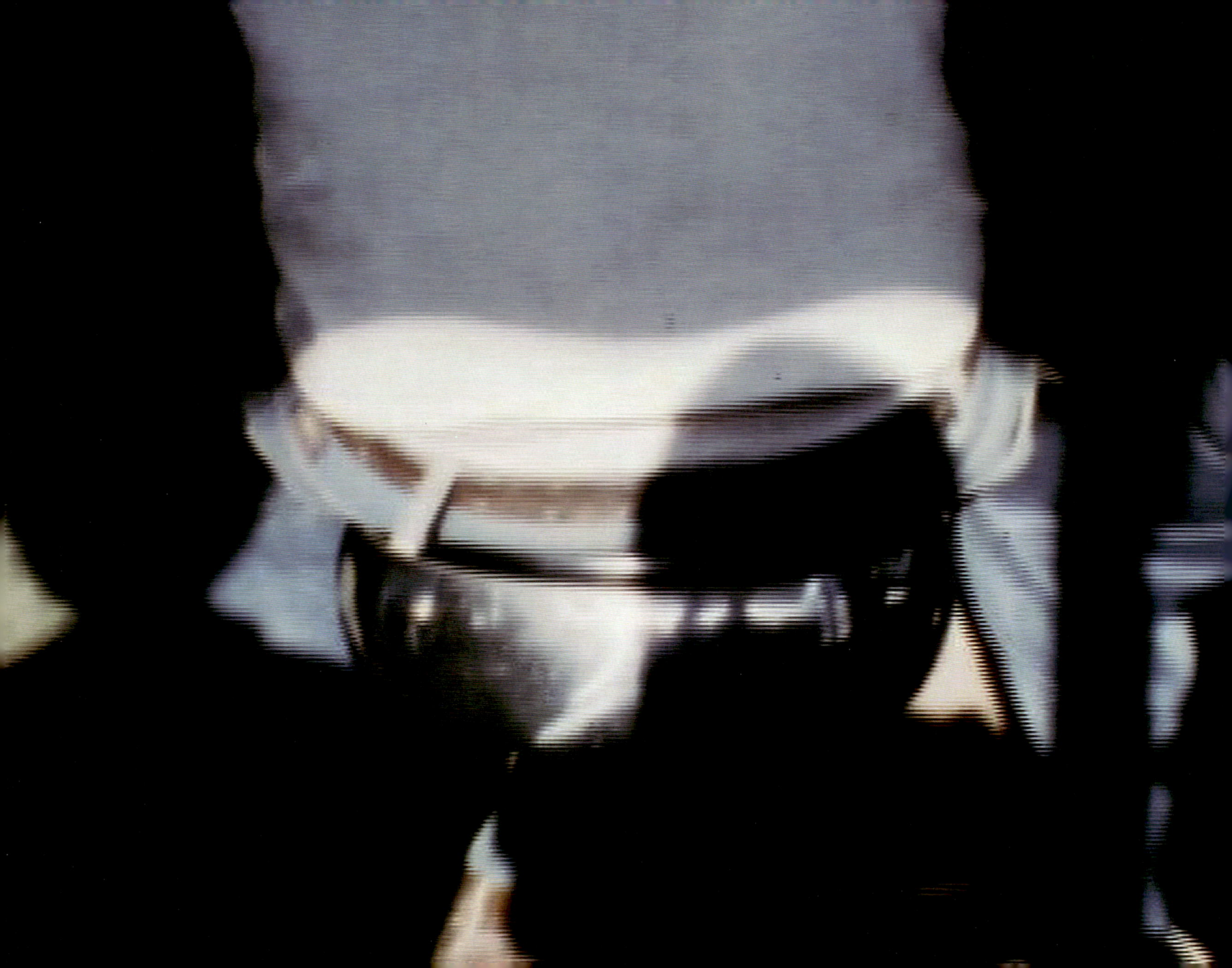

Paul Ingram

Hamburg Inn, 1967

I first entered the Hamburg Inn Number 2 in the Fall of 1967. I was a young hippy, out from Washington D.C., to become a famous writer at Iowa's world famous Writer's Workshop. There I found quite a number of Iowa folks eating what appeared to be enormous cookies, served on hamburger buns with hamburger style trappings. What they were I had no idea, but I didn't want one. Maybe a bite of someone else's. It bore a resemblance to many diner-shaped restaurants I'd eaten at before, but it seemed busier, more lively than the sad little spots I'd hit before.

The servers were not the tattooed art students you find there now. They seemed to be grandmothers in their mid-fifties, who took their jobs and their customers quite seriously. They regularly called me "honey" and took quite seriously the notion of the "bottomless cup of coffee." This was, of course, long before the university town idea of coffee had changed utterly with the help of the advance machinery that came to us from Italy by way of Seattle. There were two kinds of coffee then, fresh and old. You didn't want the old if you didn't want an ulcer.

I noticed a few beautiful couples in booths, leaning toward each other over half-eaten breakfasts after nights of unimaginable—at least to me—revelry. I made a note to myself that I should try during my time in Iowa City to find myself in such a booth with one of these pretty girls. Other customers were writing in spiral notebooks with ballpoint pens. Poets? Were any of them famous? Who knew?

On my first visit, I ordered a hamburger, the house specialty I supposed from my counter seat. My server was a fiftyish woman in full 1950s style waitress regalia, a little like a high school cafeteria worker only smiling and sweet. A favorite aunt, if I'd had one. No sooner had she taken my order than a scowling man in a dirty business suit, a suit that might have been worn the previous night, during a search for whisky and subsequent adulterous sex. He still seemed a bit drunk and possibly dangerous.

Immediately he began growling to no one in particular about hippies, about their state of general filth, their unacceptable politics, the calamity they threatened to bring upon the nation he loved, mainly the fact that they looked and behaved nothing like he did. His anger escalated and his hostility began to be directed more specifically at me. I began thinking Iowa might not have been such a great idea for a young counter culture guy like me. At a certain point, ignoring him had subtracted itself from my list of options and fear of a painful and embarrassing confrontation began to loom.

At the counter— movie still

My server-- I seem to remember the name on her tag read Liz--was having none of it, though. She came over to me and asked me if I was afraid of the man sitting next to me. "Yes," I said, "I am."

"Well, I don't blame you." said Liz, "I would be too." She turned to the aggressive male beside me.

"Are you finished with your meal?" she asked. When he indicated gruffly that he was not finished with his meal, Liz made the serious kind of eye contact made by a mother confronting a danger to her offspring.

"Why don't you make the rest of your lunch to go." She did not break her eye contact and there was a still moment watched by quite a few patrons of the Hamburg Inn. She handed the man his check. He paid it and left. Everybody clapped. I smiled. Iowa City was going to be fine.

Liz shook her head. "He was sure a crabby man, wasn't he."

"Yes he was." I answered, though I might have chosen a different adjective.

Paul's Poem (from 1967)

I may be fat
and I might be thin,
but I'm going on down
to the Hamburg Inn.

I may be short
and I might be stout
but I'll turn that HamburgInn side out.

(Paul says he submitted his poem to the Burg numerous times but claims he never got a response.)

Paul Ingram is the entertaining and highly well-read book buyer for Prairie Lights book store.

Showing off tips

Ralph Cap

Hamburg Inn No. 2 Tales

I worked at Hamburg Inn No. 2 from 1962 to 1965, or thereabouts. I started as a dishwasher and eventually waited tables and cooked burgers, typically working the late afternoon and evening hours. The coworkers that I can recall are Hopie Rhodes, Helen and her daughter Carolyn, Charlotte and her daughter Carol, Jackie De France, Lydia, Mary Ann, Lois, Marlys, Annie Wray, Ed Fitzpatrick and his brother Dennis, Rob, Kathy, Cathy, much of the Ellis family, being Arlene and her daughters Judy and Nancy, and sons Richard and Gary. Judy Ellis and I occasionally worked as a tag team on Sunday afternoons when the place became packed. She would handle the grill work and I would prepare the buns in the order that they were taken from customers. There was a protocol for handling regular burgers versus cheeseburgers. Cheeseburgers had the top portion of the bun facing down, the inside facing down, on the narrow wooden counter in front of the grill, while regular burgers had the top portion face up.

Life was never dull at Hamburg. If the customers weren't a source of entertainment we became the source. During slow winter evenings a snowball fight might break out amongst the employees, sometimes outdoors and sometimes indoors. These snowball fights usually startled the few customers present at the time. On another occasion, when life at work was slow, it precipitated another prank. Mary Ann used to drive one of the older bug-eyed Renaults. One day she parked it at a meter in front of Hamburg Inn. Richard Ellis and I went outdoors and bounced the car—it was light enough—out of the parking spot onto the sidewalk area between the meters. So, there it was, on the sidewalk, as if some inebriated person had parked it there, fenced in by the meters.

My two favorite meals were vegetable burgers and Annie Wray's delicious chicken. The homemade soups and chili were always tasty. The conversion from real live potatoes for fries to processed, frozen ones occurred around this time. The change was not widely accepted initially but eventually became the routine. Breakfast was not served all day as it is now, unless business was slow.

It was a pleasure to work for Fritz and his wife Fran. A few times I would ask a favor of Fritz and he always gladly obliged.

Greg

Once I came up with the idea of providing a succulent steak dinner for my girlfriend, but did not have the facilities where I was rooming to prepare such a meal. So I asked Fritz if I could have access to the Hamburg Inn kitchen before normal working hours to prepare the meal and be done and out of the way before work started. He saw no problem with this arrangement and all went well. At that time Hamburg Inn did not open on Sunday until mid-afternoon, so it allowed me time to fix the meal and not interfere with employees when they showed up for work. Fritz had a scurried gait at work. I don't recall ever seeing him walk at a normal pace, he always seemed in a hurry, and he probably was, always doing something there.

Adrian Flatt was the only customer that received special attention on Sundays. Sunday afternoons were especially busy because the dorms didn't serve meals that day, or at least not in the afternoons and evenings. So the nearby dorm crowd packed the place to the gills. Dr. Flatt, I think he was employed by the U of I hospitals, would call in his order and request grilled onions for his burgers. Special requests were routinely denied on those busy Sundays, except for Dr. Flatt. I don't know how he managed to be the exception, but we gladly obliged him and he was always grateful for the gesture. He had an English accent and was possibly from the UK.

August 2011

We just asked each other, Do we want to go to some culinary institute in New York City to learn about this, or do we want to go to a local diner in Iowa—the capital of the egg…and the decision was unanimous. So here we are. Jim Lindsay, writer, director, and producer of the History Channel episode of Modern Marvels, as quoted in Harrington, *The Daily Iowan*, December 2008

Adam cutting a pie

Hamburg Inn Reuben Omelet

2 to 3 ounces thin-sliced corned beef
1/2 cup sauerkraut, rinsed and well drained
Non-stick spray coating
2 beaten eggs
2 ounces sliced or shredded Swiss cheese

1. In a medium skillet, heat the thin-sliced corned beef and sauerkraut. Do not mix.
2. Spray a large skillet with non-stick spray coating. (For best results, also use a skillet with a non-stick surface.) Heat over medium heat. Add the eggs, spreading them to form a rectangle (about 9 x 7 inches).
3. Down the center of the omelet, sprinkle the cheese, then layer the sauerkraut on top of the corned beef.
4. When egg looks firm, fold the two sides over the filling. Flip omelet to cook other side.
5. Serve with additional cheese, if you like. Makes 1 omelet that serves 1.

To trim some cholesterol from this omelet recipe use 1/2 cup of an egg substitute in place of the 2 eggs, then cook as directed.

Thomas Leverett

Saturday Morning

In the seventies lots of restaurants had smoking sections and non-smoking sections, and being allergic to smoke I looked for the non-. But when a restaurant was always full like Hamburg Inn #2 was on Saturday mornings, I had to take what I could get and besides, I loved the smell of pancakes and cooked bacon and eggs. One day, when it was snowing hard outside, I couldn't find the no-smoking signs because of the crowds of people, so I started looking for ashtrays on the tables to figure that out. I realized I would be lucky to get any seat at all, but fortunately I found a friend with a rare empty seat, and was able to join him.

My seat appeared to be between the smoking and non-smoking areas, but no matter, I ordered my breakfast and started talking to my friend, who was well into eating his. Fortunately my seat was facing the Linn Street window where I could see people coming and going; it was a lively mix. The Burg drew in the entire North side and that's what I loved about it; there were poets, musicians, couples, people I knew, people I didn't. Everyone got along well.

Often there were people waiting to get a table and since people often knew each other, they would have conversations across the room or would walk over and talk to each other about the weekend's events. In an animated conversation one guy grabbed the ashtray off our table where we weren't using it and took it over to where he was discussing a poetry event with someone. I remember wondering if this would change the boundaries of the smoking section.

I got my omelet, whole-wheat toast and home fries, and my friend started telling me about the actualists, a group of poets around town, some of whom I knew. Apparently they were a kind of anti-Writer's Workshop. Whereas the workshop poets were academic and proud of it, he said, actualists believed that you shouldn't have to know Greek mythology to appreciate poetry; poetry should be about everyday things that are accessible to everyone. Like an ashtray, he said, holding up ours, which the guy had just returned.

With that my friend paid his bill and left, and was quickly replaced by another friend who shook the snow off his boots and sat in his seat. The breakfast was delicious; the comment was lost in the clang of dishes and forgotten until later. Even now, I've never seen a

1970s movie still

poem about an ashtray, haven't even seen an ashtray in many years. I remember the breakfast, though, I remember those well. But I admit some of the details are a little hazy.

June 2011

Thomas Leverett lives in Carbondale, IL, teaches ESL and writes short stories and haiku. He lived in and around Iowa City from 1975-1986.

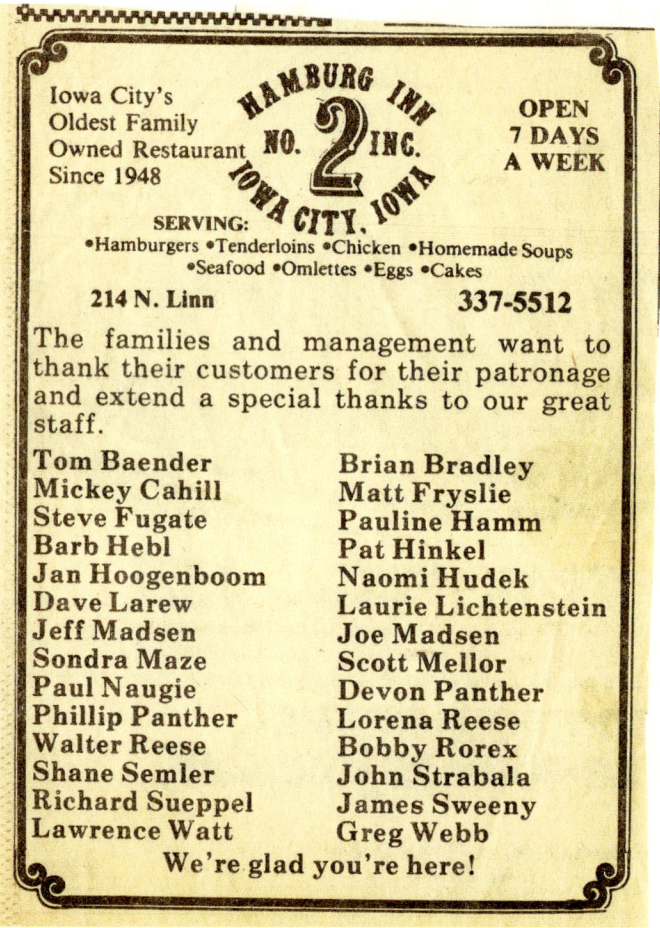

1970s movie still

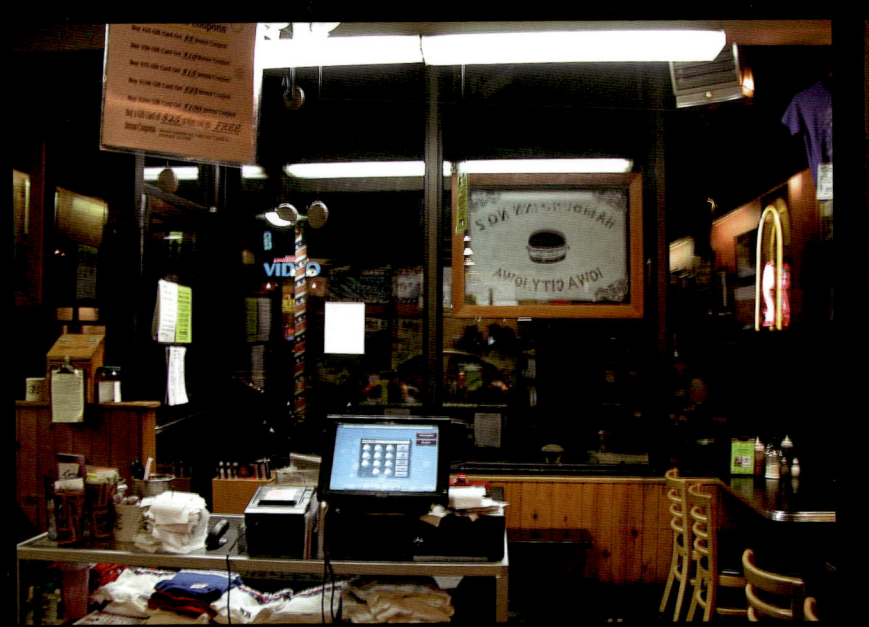

At Night

Barbara Yates

Five Ways Out

(for Mindy, Karen, Colleen, Mark & Sascha)
Let me beat the drum slowly for your
Light step;
My rhubarb wine hint of Spring and the
Rituals of the newborn.
Bubble-gum anarchists,
Search your attic for silver dreams.
If the sun rises, wake me with a shout.

Winner of the Poetry in the Buses Contest, 1977

I was one of the founders of Emma Goldman Clinic, went to law school, had my own law office and wrote poetry...all in iowa city between 1970-1977.....i won morty's Spirit that Moves Us poetry in the buses contest in 1977 and did many poetry readings when i was there...I was also Morty's attorney, and correspondingly, he was my poetry advisor....we often met at H.I.#2....i also am friends with many other people in IC and when i visit, we have to make a nostalgic stop at HI...

Now i seem to remember showing Morty the poem in my law office, and he said this could work; but i met him at #2 and he cut one of the lines and rearranged it to read the way it does....an improvement partially wrought by Hamburg Inn #2 coffee and i think there was a cheese omelet involved somewhere in there, too....HI#2 thus played a role in my formation a a poet, not to mention all the other hats I wore...we knew HI; we knew it was safe, warm, comfortable there; we knew we could create, relax, cry, laugh, revise, plot, scheme, and go back to after a long spell away from IC....

Dave Morice

Manners at the Burg

The waitress brought my breakfast plate
And set it on the table.
I said, as kindly as I could,
"Why, thank you, Mable."

"No, no," she said in sugary tones
Like honey poured in tea,
And chirped with emphasis, "Thank you
For thanking me."

Ah, maple syrup is far less sweet,
So what else could I do?
I said, "Thank you for thanking me
For thanking you."

Then Mable's voice went Sweet 'n' Low.
"No, no, thank you," said she,
"For thanking me for thanking you
For thanking me."

1972

When Dr. Alphabet was asked about editing his work with his friend Mary Jo at the Hamburg Inn on a weekly basis—and eating pancakes—he replied that "There is more to this than meets the eye. For four years, I've met with Mary Jo Dane once a week at HI and eat sweet potato pancakes. However, I bring various poems for her to read and comment on. She used to teach at Southeast, where my son Danny went to school and had her as a teacher. She recognized Danny's last name and asked, 'Is your father Dr. Alphabet?' He said yes, and she asked if I would come in and teach a class for a day. I offered instead to do a week-long poetry class and workshop to her students (as I used to do through the Iowa Arts Council.) After Danny went to City High, Mary Jo asked me if I would do the same thing the following year, and I agreed to do that--because it was so much fun to work with her and her kids. I went in for four years in a row, and would've gone in every year after that, but she retired. That wasn't the end of our friendship. Not only is she an excellent teacher, but an excellent editor, too. She helped me edit some of my books, articles, and poems at Hamburg Inn. Her comments were extremely helpful."

"Now for a romantic turn. Mary Jo and I got to know each other during those four year sweet potato pancake poetry meetings, and we became very good friends. On Feb 13, 2011, I mentioned to her that I needed some help straightening up my apartment for a visitor. I didn't ask her to help, but she volunteered to come over and work on it with me. As it turned out, after all those pancake years, we realized that day that we were no longer friends--because we realized that those pancake years had led up to a romance, and that's where we are today. Teacher plus poet plus pancake = love."

One of perhaps many romantic stories that have occurred at the Hamburg Inn over the years.

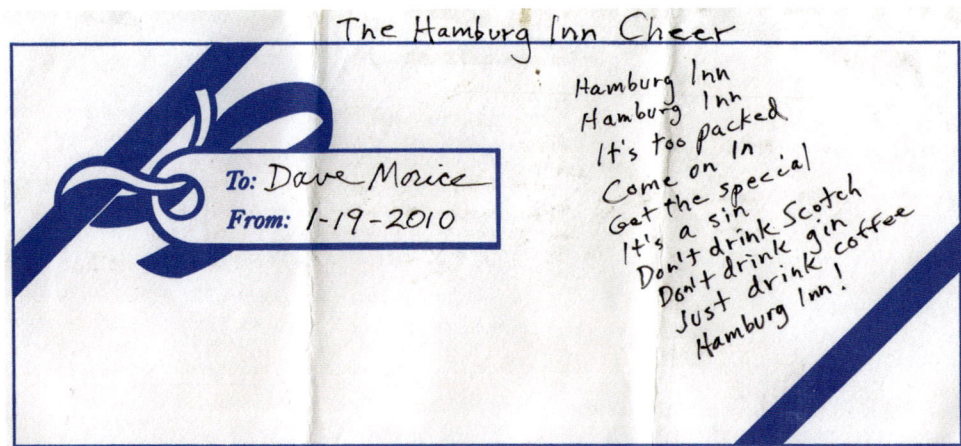

The Paper Plate Special For Hamburg Inn, the tastiest place in town!

As I sit here
facing a midnight breakfast,
I see the world
in a paper plate.
The world is one egg
sunny-side up
shimmering
in the night.

The table shakes
when I kick it.
I see the world shake
in the paper plate,
where I could never live
since I'm too big
to inhabit the yolk
of a golden world.

O where? O who?
O what am I doing here
at the witching hour
when the stars twinkle
in so many eyes?

Is the moon an egg
before its cracked
for the paper plate?
The night isn't young!

That's one of those
mysteries of nature,
where time gives an age
to truth, youth, and beauty.
These things are here, too,
at The Hamburg Inn, although
sometimes they're just side orders.

If you pop the yolk
of the delicate egg,
the world appears to melt
across the paper plate.
It's very special
because it's 45¢
and because of so many
other things—but they're on other planets.

Dave Morice/Dr. Alphabet, August 2, 1975

"Note that I have written more poems on more occasions at Hamburg Inn No. 2 than at any other place (except my home, of course)." Dr. Alphabet

Mary Jo Dane

At the Burg
(after Walt Whitman)

At the Burg, I loafe and invite my soul,
I lean and loafe at my ease observing a sweet potato pancake.
Nature without check with original energy,
I am mad for it to be in contact with me.
Since every atom belonging to me as good belongs to you,
You wanna come, too?

"One day, a year ago or so, Mary Jo wrote a delightful poem, a Walt Whitman parody, inviting me to come to the Burg that day."
Dr. Alphabet

Chris at the register

Liz Sanders

There is an undeniable heart and soul of the Hamburg Inn. It has created a sense of community and is a staple in Iowa City's history. It has inspired and fed generations. In 2001, I began my story with the Hamburg as a part-time dishwasher-hopeful waitress, never with the thought I would be part of the next generation. Years as a waitress and supervisor, then assistant manager, now general manager, I've grown and changed as much as the Hamburg has, but one thing has remained the same: I've always had fun, loved my job and looked forward to whatever was to come next in the busy life of the
Hamburg. From my managers, Steve Fugate and Shonda Hitchcock, and of course the owner, Dave Panther, at the
Hamburg I've worked for some of the most genuine and good hearted people I've ever met. I am thankful for my opportunity to continue the tradition that Dave's father has passed on. That is, to carry on all the stories that there are to tell and create some of the best homemade food Iowa City has ever feasted on.

"As far as speed goes, we can't match McDonald's," David says. "As far as variety goes, we can match just about anybody." Heth, *Iowa City Press-Citizen,* October 1983

Liz Sanders taking an order around 2003

Panther said the in-house grinding of the meat is the key to the Hamburg Inn hamburger... the restaurant receives shipments of meat twice a week. A staff member feeds the meat through a grinder twice before forming it into 6-ounce balls. Jennings, *Cedar Rapids Gazette*, September 2003

Juan Cormona, long-time Hamburg Inn butcher, forms ground beef into patties

Gary Sanders wrote the *Road Food and Good Food* authors, Jane and Michael Stern, before their series became well known. He urged them to try the Hamburg Inn saying, "I've traveled in 48 states and the Hamburg Inn No. 2 is the best restaurant of its type I know." They did visit the diner and featured it in their second, 1986, edition; they said "...the pieces de resistance were American fried potatoes. Big chunky spuds heaped on the grill, a cup an order, sprinkled with grease, and fried until crusty. Delicious!"

Paris at work

Michael Knock

The Burg: Three Meals, Six Hours and Countless 'Lucky Cows'

I moved to Iowa City in 1998. Ostensibly, I came here for the graduate program in journalism at the University of Iowa, but the Hamburg Inn played at least a small role in my decision as well. I knew the Burg well from years of driving from my home in northwest Iowa to South Bend, Indiana. Every trip through Iowa City included a stop at Prairie Lights, coffee at The Java House, and breakfast at The Hamburg Inn. I visited often enough to even develop a small crush on a member of the wait staff. Yes, my usual was an Iowa omelet with hash browns and a side of unrequited love.

Flash forward 13 years, and it has been months since I've been to the Hamburg. I decide to make up for lost time by hitting my old haunt for breakfast, lunch and dinner all in the same day. After walking the dog and grabbing a notebook and pen, I head over to 214 N. Linn Street on a humid Monday in August to see if the place still has the same appeal.

Breakfast: Iowa Omelet with Hash Browns (and zombies)
It's 8:05 a.m. My goal for the morning is get some coffee, a little breakfast and to do some people watching. Under different circumstances the latter activity might be considered a bit rude and possibly even borderline creepy, but I'm a writer. I have a notebook. That makes it A-OK.

I want to see without being seen; to be a fly on the wall. Such a thing may not be possible. As playwright David Mamet once said "In a restaurant one is both observed and unobserved. Joy and sorrow can be displayed and observed 'unwittingly,' the writer scowling naively and the diners wondering, 'What the hell is he doing?'"

His point is proven all too well. As I move in to snag a spot along the counter, a friend spots me and waves me over. So much for being unobserved. I put on a smile, tuck my notebook away and sit down.

Our conversation is breezy and ranges from Iowa river towns – "There was a time when towns like Dubuque and even Keokuk were nice places to live" - to high school girls' basketball - "I once told (Des Moines Register columnist) Donald Kaul that he killed six-on-six (basketball) in Iowa." I smile and nod. I loved six-on-six girls' basketball. I can name every state champion from 1974-1993. But I digress.

The waiter – a nice young guy with brown hair and glasses – comes and takes my order: an Iowa omelet, but instead of ham I ask for sausage. He doesn't blink an eye at my special order. I also ask for coffee, and he dutifully returns with a cup. He stops by a lot over the next couple of hours. Every time my cup gets half-empty, the guy comes and fills it up again. God bless America.

My plan for the morning was to avoid conversation and simply observe people, but that's nearly impossible at the Hamburg. I find myself being drawn in to the talk. Maybe it's the coffee. Maybe it's the fact that I'm sitting at the counter. Maybe it's the fact that the mere mention of girls' basketball always piques my interest.

Still, I manage to pick up a few details here and there. It's amazing what people will do when they think no one is watching. Queen's "Don't Stop Me Now" is playing on the stereo in the kitchen, and I notice that when he's not filling my cup with coffee, my waiter is pantomiming the scene from the movie "Shawn of the Dead" where the characters fight off zombies with pool cues. I stifle a smile. I think he's seen the movie once or twice.

I turn back to my friend who is now showing me old photos from Iowa City. We look at the Astro Theatre – now a bank – and I remark that I saw the last movie ever shown at there, Madonna's "Truth or Dare," back in the summer of 1991. He is unimpressed. He pays his bill, wraps up a small scrap of meat in a napkin and tells the waitress it's for his dog.

"Just one of them?" she asks. "What about the others?"

It's 8:40 a.m.

Lunch: Chicken Bites and French Fries with Barbecue Sauce (and lucky cows)
I think of author William Least Heat-Moon every time I walk into a new diner. Least Heat-Moon famously wrote in his book *Blue Highways* that you could tell the quality of a diner by counting the number of calendars on the wall. "No calendars – same as an interstate pit stop; one calendar – preprocessed food assembled in New Jersey; two calendars – only if fish trophies are present; three calendars – can't miss on the farm-boy breakfasts; four calendars – try the ho-made pie; five calendars – keep it under your hat, or they'll franchise."

The Hamburg doesn't seem to fit anywhere on Least Heat-Moon's score sheet. Over lunch I scan the room looking for calendars, but I see none, and this is no interstate pit stop. Maybe Iowa City's equivalent is the number of politicians' photos on the walls. The Burg scores big there. From my perch along the counter I spot congressmen and former congressmen, a US senator and not one, not two but three presidents. The booth along the northwest wall even has a plaque designating it as the place where Ronald Reagan sat during an Iowa City visit back in 1992.

The politics on the walls are matched by a level of politics at the tables. Earlier in the day I noticed a man in his mid-20s – definitely a graduate student – reading the *New York Times* over a cup of coffee. Now, two guys to my right catch my eye…or, more specifically, my ear.

"I have no trouble killing and eating free range cattle," says a guy wearing an "Imagine Peace" T-shirt to his friend in a Cubs hat. "Those cows have it so awesome. They get to hang out in the sunshine all day just eating and sleeping."

I want to hear more about lucky cows, but I am distracted by a loud belch coming from the customer to my left. He just finished off a burger and fries, and now he is in the middle of a chocolate malt. He punctuates slurps of the malt with periodic burps. It's a little mean, but I start keeping track. It's 1:40 p.m.

Imagine Peace is now talking to his friend about the debt-ceiling debate that dominated political news much of the summer. "You should care about it," Imagine Peace says. "Your student loans are going to go up. You know that, right?"

Cubs Hat doesn't respond. Maybe his student loans are already paid off. Or maybe he just wants to finish his lunch. He nods his head and continues eating.

Belch. I check my watch. It's now 1:53 p.m.

Imagine Peace moves on to a conversation about the Iowa caucuses. "You've gotta get involved in the Iowa caucuses," he says. "They're like Iowa's primary."

Belch. It's 1:58 p.m.

The waitress comes over to check on the belching guy. From their banter, I can tell he must be a regular customer.

"How was everything today?" she asks, and from the tone of her voice I can tell that the question isn't just a formality. She really wants to know, and now so do I.

"The fries were really good," Belching Guy says. "But they could have been a little less crispy."

"You mean they were burned?" she asks with a slight touch of concern.

"No, they were just a little crispier than I like," Belching Guy responds. "Otherwise, they were good."
I look down at the few remaining fries on my own plate. Belching Guy has a point. I thought my fries were too crispy too. It's 2:18 p.m.

Dinner: Grilled Cheese with Ranch Dressing on the Side (and Michele Bachman)
I've convinced my husband, also named Michael (yes, it's confusing), to join me at the Burg for dinner. We are sitting in the coveted Reagan Booth on the 19th anniversary of the former president's visit, and Michael is scanning the photos along the wall. In one autographed shot, Nancy and Ronald Reagan both smile down at our table.

"I never noticed how much bigger her head was than his," Michael remarks. "She looks just like a doll."

I nod. While I enjoy the conversation, I am still here to do a job. As I scan the restaurant I see that the dinner crowd is different from those I dined with at breakfast and lunch. More people seem to be eating alone tonight. Some are on their cell phones while others read newspapers.

By 7:20 the place is so quiet that I can clearly hear conversations across the room. A man and woman are standing at the cash register waiting for a take-out order. "This sure is a great place to eat when you don't want anything fancy," he says to her. She nods and pays the bill.

I agree. While I would never order rib-eye at the Burg, my grilled cheese was tasty. It came with fries, and the kitchen must have gotten Belching Guy's message. They were definitely less crispy than they had been that afternoon. Just right, Goldilocks might say.

We move to the counter to pay, and I notice the famous Coffee Bean Caucus next to the register. In all my years in Iowa City, I've never participated in this institution, so I pick up a few beans and drop them into my jars of choice. Michael does the same.

"There sure are a lot of votes in here for Michele Bachman," Michael remarks to the waitress taking our money. "That's really scary."

The waitress pauses and thinks for a second. "You know, everyone who comes through here says the same thing. I don't know who keeps putting these beans in here."

It's 7:36 p.m.

Michael Knock has written the weekly food column, "Cooking Class," for the *Iowa City Press-Citizen* since 2004. He also teaches history and composition at Clarke University in Dubuque, and he is ashamed to admit that he has never tried a pie shake.

Polly doing an omelet demo for the History Channel crew

Hamburg Inn #2
July 1, 1976

Les Finken, left, has been a patron since 1974, when he was an undergraduate student. He got interested in computer science and eventually worked in the Department of Information Technology Services at the University of Iowa. He often walks over for lunch; he said he likes the range of newspapers that end up in the box up front.

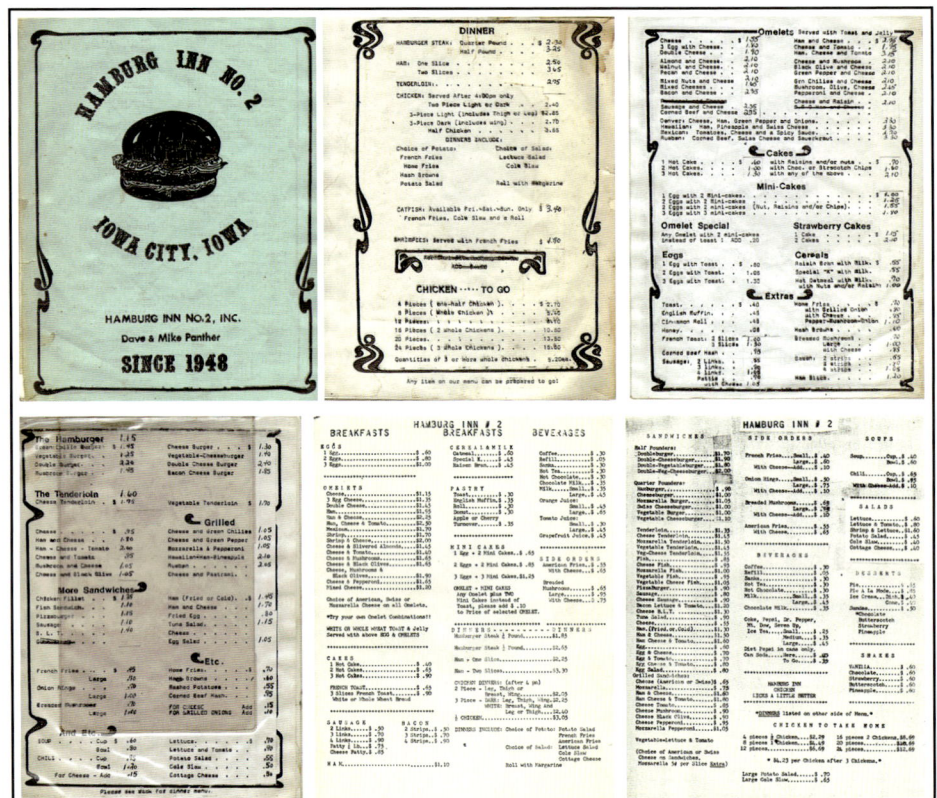

I grew up a block away on N. Linn St. so my fondest memories of the Burg are from my childhood. I spent many hours there with my friends and family. It was one of our homes away from home...including Pagliai's of course. However, I did work there for a year in '83—'84. From peeling potatoes for those awesome deluxe home fries to endless dishes and pots and pans.
I enjoyed the interesting conversations with the staff and patrons. The staff had been there for 20, 30 years or were just passing-thru students, but all were entertaining, eccentric and deserving of your retrospective. I remember one older gentleman that studied stocks and bonds and finance and he would come in after the dinner rush and hang out at the old counter near the grill until closing. He would throw out little tidbits of economic wisdom if anyone was interested but he never pushed his passion. There were/are so many brilliant people in Iowa City and many have claimed Hamburg Inn #2 as their living room and social center. David A. Larew, correspondence

Talia getting off work

It was this unknown man (whom
I tried to identify), writing at a table
one afternoon, that suggested to
me that in addition to satisfying
appetites, there might be a great
number of stories, poems, sketches,
and ideas that have been generated
in this small space. Then bigger
themes started scrolling by—
emotions and needs felt here like
hope, ambition, sadness, fear,
remembrance, attraction, bitterness,
stillness, loneliness, anger, loyalty,
panic... perhaps all the emotions.
And some were written down and
some will be.   M.S.

Leaving the Fold: It saddens us when our people need to move on, but we realize time does not stand still even at the H.I. Due to scheduling 3 weeks ahead of time please try to give us at least 3 weeks notice you are quitting. People who culminate their time here in a professional manner will usually be welcomed back.

Undated Employee Handout hanging on the wall:

Bibliography

Newspaper quotes that appear in brown type throughout the book are as follows:

Bello, Deidre. "NBC show features Iowa City diner." *Iowa City Press-Citizen*, (January 27, 2005)

Binegar, Erika. "Biden chides Democratic leaders; Delaware senator visits Hamburg in I.C.." *Cedar Rapids Gazette*, (August 21, 2007)

Binegar, Erika. "Popped inn: Ex-president springs breakfast surprise on restaurant in I.C." *Cedar Rapids Gazette*, (November 28, 2007)

Binegar, Erika. "The results are the same; Coffee Bean Caucus increases attention on Iowa City hangout." *Cedar Rapids Gazette*, (December 8, 2008)

Binegar, Erika. "Still flipping after all these years: The Hamburg Inn general manager will celebrate his 25th anniversary at the Iowa City icon." *The Daily Iowan*, November 15, 2005)

Cedar Rapids Gazette staff writer. "The Hamburg Inn's a 38-year Iowa City tradition." *Cedar Rapids Gazette*, (May 28, 1986)

Daly, Dan. "Ode on a Greasy Spoon." webmaster@hamburginn.com, 04/23/09 01:30 PM

Fiegen, Kathryn. "Edwards makes best of weather; Stranded, he pays visit to Hamburg." *Iowa City Press-Citizen,* (December 12, 2007)

Fiegen, Kathryn. "Having breakfast with Bill; Ex-president makes visit to Hamburg Inn." *Iowa City Press-Citizen*, (November 28, 2007)

Geake, Sara. "Burg Inn to hit the bright lights of 'West Wing.'" *The Daily Iowan*, (January 21, 2005)

Harrington, Mary. "Local diner eggs on history." *The Daily Iowan*, (December 9, 2008)

Heth, Jerald. "Ode to a greasy spoon: Hamburg No. 1 is gone." *Des Moines Register,* (May, 1978)

Heth, Jerry. "'Nobody's out of place here' Panther family marks 35 years of service at downtown's Hamburg Inn No. 2." *Iowa City Press-Citizen*, (October 3, 1983)

Hibbs, Robert G. *Iowa City: A Sense of Place*, Iowa City Press-Citizen (2001)

Howe, Kathryn. "The Sit-Down with Laurel Snyder." *Little Village*, (November, 2008)

Jennings, Amy. "'The Burg' celebrates 55 by giving to customers." *Cedar Rapids Gazette*, (September 12, 2003)

Kerr, Drew. "Burg Inn relishes its political role." *The Daily Iowan*, (November 1, 2004)

Kucharski, Zack. "Hamburg Inn goes Hollywood." *Cedar Rapids Gazette*, (January 21, 2005)

Meyer, Diana Lambdin. "Corn Belt Caucus." *AAA Living*, (January/February, 2008)

Mohr, Lisa. "The best burgers in the Midwest: they're served at Hamburg Inn." *icon*, (June 15, 1995)

Olson, Henry. "Hamburg Inn: tried and true." *The Daily Iowan*

Panther, Dave. *The Burg Diner Liner*, (June 2008-continuing.)

Pracht, Adam. "'West Wing' to feature Hamburg." *Iowa City Press-Citizen*, (January 20, 2005)

Richter, Shawna. "Iowa City restaurant stars in television's 'West Wing'." *The Hawk Eye*, Burlington, Iowa, (January 23, 2005)

Risch, Karen. "Hamburg Inn does more than just survive after fire." *View from The Hawk's Eye/Hawkeye Food Systems Inc.*, (Summer, 1994)

Shim, Grace. "Waitress' 40-year career nearly over; Hamburg Inn's 'last one of the old ones' retires." *Iowa City Press-Citizen*, (March 31, 1999)

Sklar, Morty and Darrell Gray, eds. *The Actualist Anthology*, The Spirit That Moves Us Press (1977)

Snyder, Laurel. "I have an MFA in poetry, may I take your order?" *Little Village*: Iowa City's News and Culture Magazine, Vol. 1, Issue 12. (February, 2002)

Snyder, Laurel. *Inside the Slidy Diner,* Tricycle Press (2008)

Staff. "Pressure cooker explodes, one injured." *Iowa City Press-Citizen*, (December 21, 1948)

Stern, Jane and Michael Stern. *Road Food and Good Food,* Alfred A. Knopf (1986*)*

Sunderbruch, Jude. "Hamburg Inn closes down following fire." *The Daily Iowan,* (April, 1994)

Vilsack, Christie. "Main Street: Hamburg Inn No. 2." *Mt. Pleasant News*, (April 3, 1991)

Wells, John. The West Wing [script of episode 13]. "King Corn." Warner Brothers Entertainment Inc., (November 8, 2004)

Wilson, Jennifer. "Hamburg Inn No. 2" in "Esquire's Breakfast Part 2: Eating Out; Our Unranked, Incomplete, and Unimpeachable List of the Best Breakfasts Woodin, Heather Sloman.

"Happy Birthday, Burg! Iowa City's landmark greasy spoon turns 45." *Cedar Rapids Gazette*, (September, 1994)

Woodin, Heather Sloman. "Fire fails to close down Hamburg Inn tradition." *Cedar Rapids Gazette*, (August 3, 1994)

Wundram, Bill. "An affectionate salute to Iowa's 'greasy spoon'." *Quad-City Times*, (September 5, 1993)

Wundram, Bill. "A greasy spoon's Coffee Bean Poll." *Quad-City Times*, (October 10, 2004)

My thanks to all the people who made this book possible: to the writers who generously contributed stories and essays and the staff who allowed me to photograph them when both of us were on the run; to Morty Sklar, Marvin Bell, Carl Klaus, and Ken for their encouragement, suggestions and contacts; to Mary Bennett at the State Historical Society of Iowa for the use of her home movie; to Beverly Dolezal for assisting with photos and stories of Mrs. Vander Linden; to Dave Morice for his set of drawings and poems and Christopher Ford for his photographs; to the graphic artists, guests, Panther family, and, finally, to Dave, who hired me.

Staff in my photos:

Adam Angstead
Chris Borders
Brittany Burggraaf
Juan Cormona
Polly Crist
Joe Dunkle
Robert Ajax Ehl
Greg Flanagan
Christopher Ford
James Gust
Ben Judas
Talia Meidlinger
Mike Mills
Luke Peterson
Emily Qual
Paris Roby
Liz Sanders

Panther said another measure of the restaurant's popularity are T-shirt sales, which began in the 1970s. He said many patrons relay stories of seeing the solid-colored shirts with the restaurant's logo in locations around the globe, including a bed and breakfast in France and an expedition in South America. Jennings, *Cedar Rapids Gazette,* September 2003

At Hamburg Inn

they serve lunch

at dinnertime

and they serve dinner

at lunchtime

At Hamburg Inn

there's a counter

"... thirty-five, thirty-six, thirty-seven..."

Thank you, counter

At Hamburg Inn

I sit at the table

next to the door

and wait for inspiration

nothing less, nothing more

but they serve breakfast

at all hours

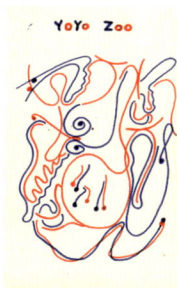

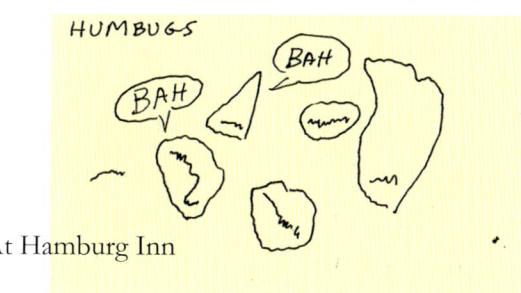

At Hamburg Inn

At Hamburg Inn

the ceiling fans

go round and round

until the air

is square and square

At Hamburg Inn

a mirror

reflects

on itself

Bill Clinton

sat at that table

and ate that burger

and won

the presidency

Dave Morice's sketches were done at the Burg around 1978; his poems are from the Poetry City Marathon, Vol. 38, *The Book of The Hamburg Inn-athon*, performed August 10, 2010 at Hamburg Inn.

At Hamburg Inn

nobody memorizes their lines

The play goes on

and

on

It's reality TV

without the TV

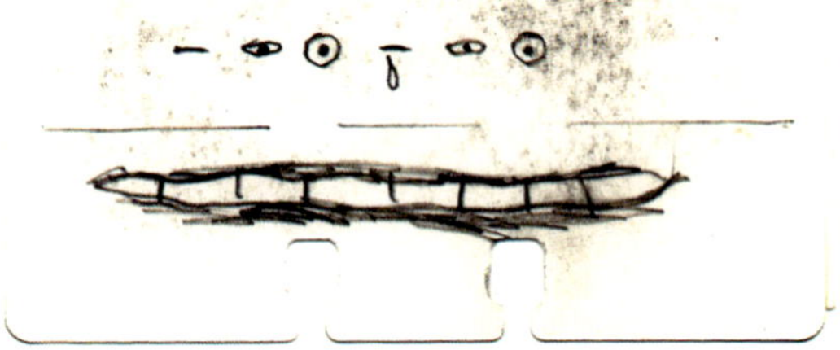

At Hamburg Inn

the hamburgers

dance on the grill

to the music

of the fries

At Hamburg Inn

the clock

on the wall

doesn't tick

It tocks

It tocks to anyone who will listen

At Hamburg Inn

the radio

yells

at the grill

At Hamburg Inn

there are two doors

One for you

and one for you

At Hamburg Inn

I'vdrunkalotofcoffee

I mean

I've drunk a lot of coffee

Back Cover: Linn Street, November 1966; the Graf Bottling Co. building on the north was purchased by ACT; since demolished